TWO YEARS ON THE WATCH

WHAT I LEARNED IN THE SECRET COLD WAR BUNKER

BRUCE RIGNEY

© 2018 BRE, Inc. All rights reserved.

Front cover photo of bunker entrance courtesy of DOATRIP.de.
Bunker doors image courtesy of Morten Jensen, Randers, Denmark.
Back cover image of the 412L Aircraft Warning & Control System
© General Electric Company and used with its permission.

ISBN-10: 1983981990

CONTENTS

Illustrations v
Preface 1
Eighty Feet Under 3
What We Were Watching. 11
What a Tangled Web We Wove 19
What Didn't Happen Actually 25
Big Wind From Washington 37
In the Line of Duty 47
The Cabinet of Curiosities. 55
Curiouser and Curiouser 63
My Big Fat Security Clearance 69
Welcome to the Neighborhood 75
My Humble Abode 83
We're Not in the U.S. Anymore 93
Skeletons in the Closets 103
Alarming Incidents. 111
A Friend in the News 129
Unlock and Load 135
Decisions Have Been Made 151
Pushing Some Buttons 159
My Last Assignment. 169
Getting Better All the Time 173
Second Thoughts 183
Acknowledgments 195

ILLUSTRATIONS

Army Missile Defense Battalions,
Air Force Radar Sites and Air Bases vi
Cutaway View of the Börfink Bunker...............vii
Nuclear Weapon Effects Calculator
Issued by the Defense Nuclear Agency viii

Army Missile Defense Battalions, Air Force Radar Sites and Air Bases

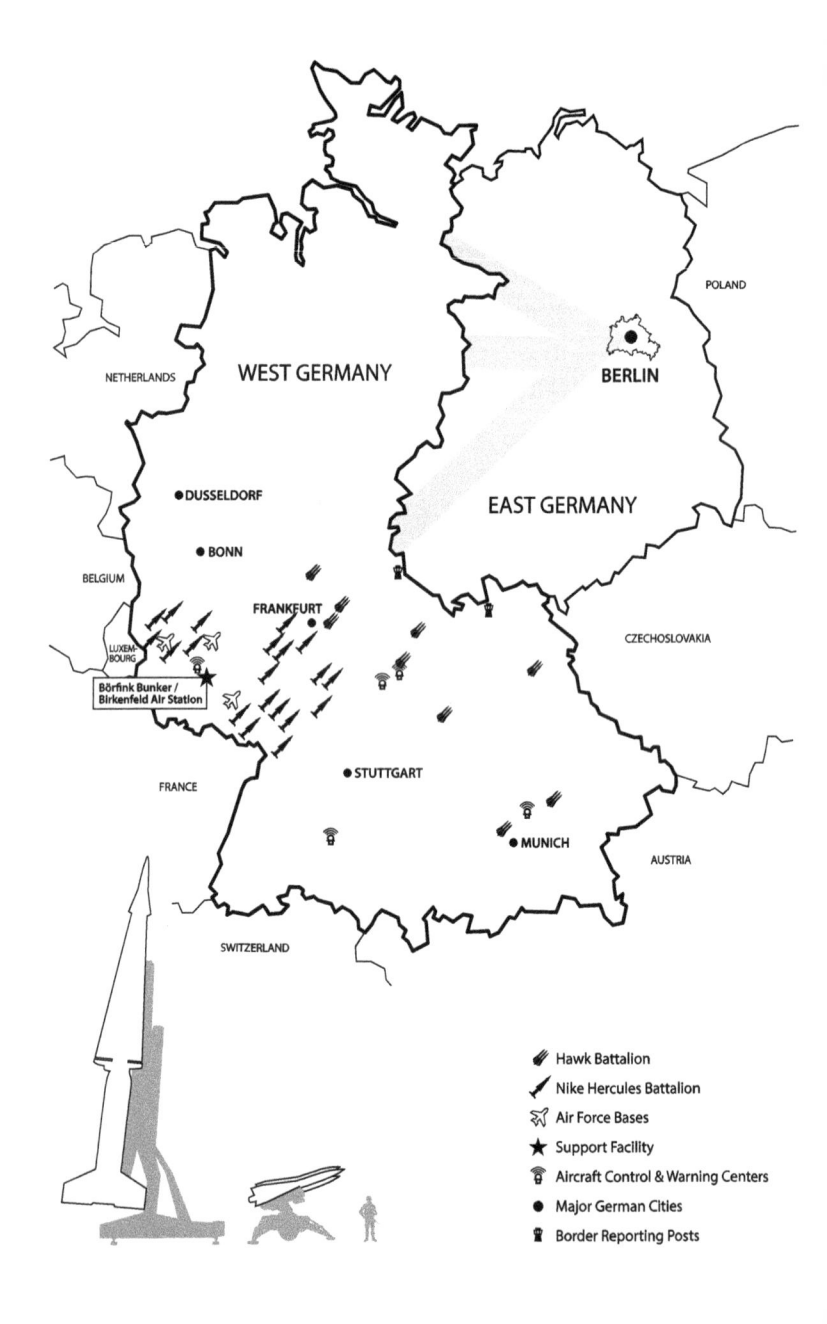

Cutaway View of the Börfink Bunker

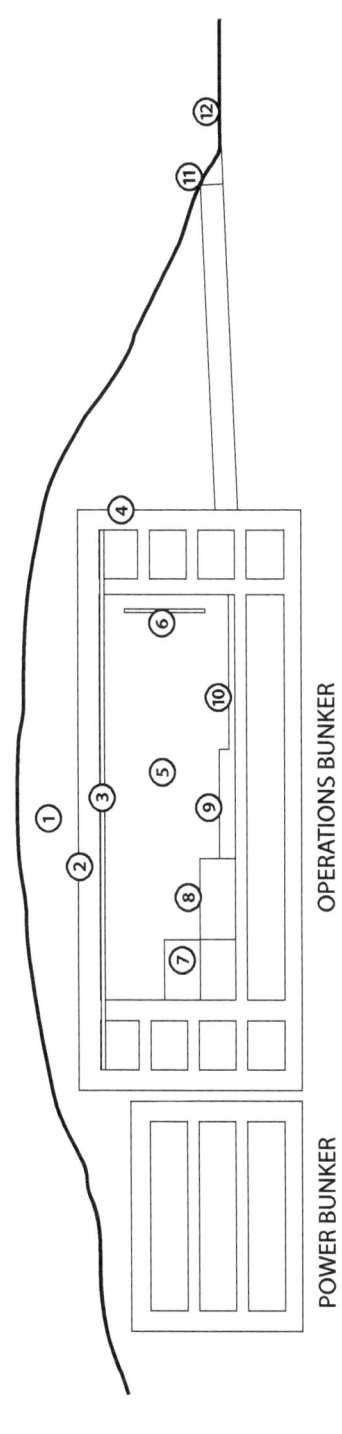

POWER BUNKER

OPERATIONS BUNKER

1. 20 feet of soil and forest growth
2. 13 feet of reinforced concrete
3. 2.5-foot-thick steel I-beam
4. 12 feet of reinforced concrete
5. SOC III main operations room
6. Master display screen
7. SOC III command dais (intelligence booth, weatherman, sector controller, German liaison and French observer)
8. U.S Army missile command staff
9. U.S. Air Force radar and control staff
10. German Air Force radar staff and German air traffic controllers
11. Entrance
12. Parking lot

Nuclear Weapon Effects Calculator
Issued by the Defense Nuclear Agency

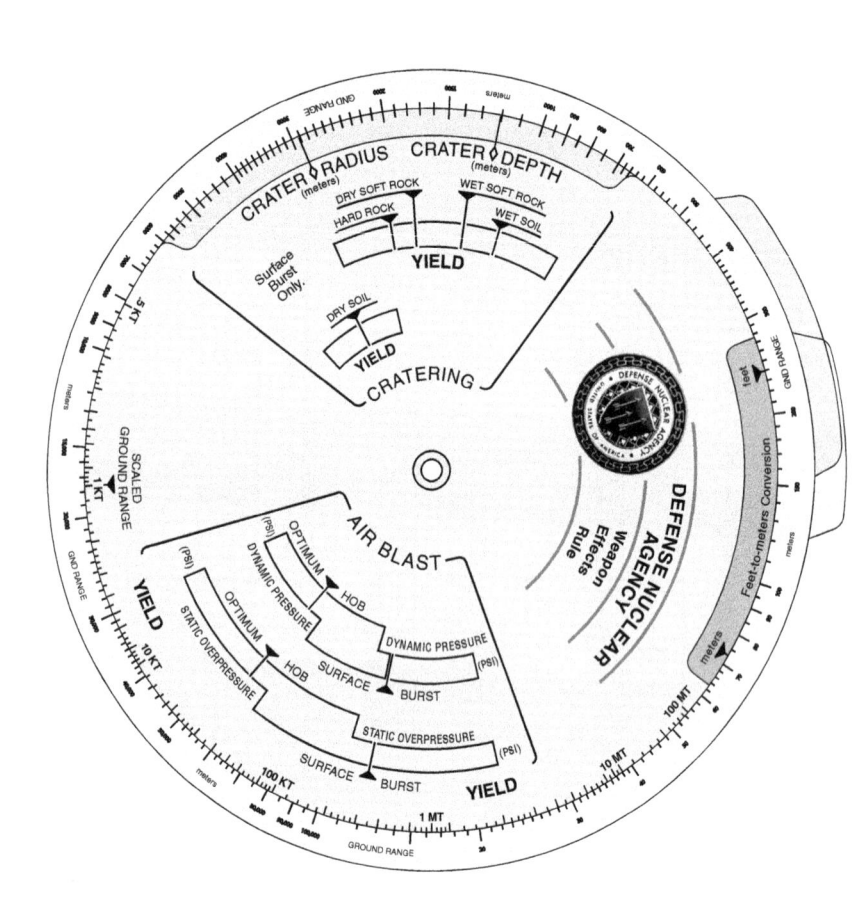

KT: kiloton bomb
MT: megaton bomb

GND: ground
HOB: height of burst

PREFACE

IN ASSEMBLING THE MATERIAL FOR this book, I was often pleasantly surprised by the clarity and detail of recollection of my U.S. Air Force service in Germany in the late 1960s. I am also indebted to the many contributors to Wikipedia and to the independent and retired former American and German military member websites that helped to jog my memory and sometimes verify and complete the details of military procedures and actions of fifty years ago.

Even if I had recalled every detail, until 2012 I would have been constrained from divulging much of the data due to security restrictions on documents and procedures that have now been released for public knowledge by the National Security Agency and the U.S. Air Force.

Many of those restrictions were lifted when the NSA declassified large portions of a four-part, top-secret history that disclosed new information about the agency's history and the role of SIGINT (Signals Intelligence) and COMINT (Communications Intelligence) during the Cold War.

Researched and written by NSA historian Dr. Thomas R. Johnson, the top-secret *History of the National Security Agency, American Cryptology during the Cold War, (1945-1989)* is a unique and invaluable study for those interested in the history of U.S. intelligence during the Cold War or for those who are interested in learning more about the role of the National Security Agency in the U.S. government.

This material can be referenced at The National Security Archive:

http://nsarchive.gwu.edu/NSAEBB/NSAEBB260/

Other restrictions were lifted with the February 1, 1998 release of the U.S. Air Force publication titled Pamphlet 14-210, Intelligence, chapter on "Information and Intelligence," located on the Internet at https://fas.org/irp/doddir/usaf/afpam14-210/

The release of these document restrictions were the result of responses to records requests allowed by amendments to the federal Freedom of Information Act. These policies were implemented in the 1990s and allowed the release of previously classified national security documents that were more than twenty-five years old and of historical interest, allowing many previously publicly unknown details about the Cold War and other historical events to be studied and discussed openly.

EIGHTY FEET UNDER

ONLY A FEW WEEKS AFTER my twenty-third birthday, I found myself eighty feet underground staring out at a wall of flickering green and red lights while being held personally responsible for the safety of Western Europe against the military might of the Soviet Union and its Warsaw Pact allies.

Having graduated from the U.S. Air Force's Air Intelligence School in Denver, Colorado, I was a recently commissioned Second Lieutenant now stationed at my first posting in West Germany crammed into a restricted-access Intelligence Watch Officer (IWO) booth on the top-level command platform of the secret, deeply undergrounded concrete bunker that housed the NATO command post known as Sector Operations Center III (SOC III).

SOC III and the U.S. Air Force's 615th Aircraft Control and Warning Squadron first occupied the Bunker in 1964 at its location near one of the highest elevations in West Germany, about thirty miles east of the Luxembourg and French borders. We were located just below the radar station and microwave relay station at the Erbeskopf, a mountain about two thousand and seven hundred feet above sea level in the Hunsrück mountain range in southwest Germany. At that height, the Erbeskopf was the highest point of German territory west of the Rhine River, making it the ideal location for the hub of a central network of air defense communications and control.

In the military, a watch system is a designation of regular periods of work that allow an assigned duty to effectively operate for twenty-four hours, seven days a week. In the intelligence field, the officer on the watch is also continuously observing and looking out for indications of hostile activity, reporting and analyzing the data or actions observed.

On my first day on the job, I had been informed that my function would be to advise the SOC III Sector Controller, the on-duty officer in charge, and through him informing the U.S. Air Forces in Europe regarding developments of any threats to Western Europe from the Soviet-controlled Warsaw Pact.

The Pact had been formed in 1955 with a treaty signed in Warsaw, Poland, that included the Soviet Union, Albania, Poland, Romania, Hungary, East Germany, Czechoslovakia, and Bulgaria as members. It stood in opposition to the member countries of the North Atlantic Treaty Organization (NATO). This western European counterpart to the Warsaw Pact had been established in 1949 and included Belgium, Canada, Denmark, France, Great Britain, Iceland, Italy, Luxembourg, the Netherlands, Norway, Portugal, the United States and West Germany.

Those were the individual players on the two opposing forces of the Cold War that were faced off at the border between West and East Germany. For my first two months on the job, I had been indoctrinated into my role as part of the command team tasked with monitoring and controlling air traffic and border defenses in Western Europe.

Outside my booth window, I viewed directly in front of me the flickering green vertical bars of light that depicted friendly aircraft and the magenta bars of the unidentified aircraft over in the Soviet zone of occupied Germany. These potentially hostile or "bogey" aircraft were being tracked by our five U.S. Air Force radar facilities spread out across southwest Germany. With each radar site having a range of about four hundred miles, we were provided with an accurate and comprehensive information network tracking air traffic across Central Europe.

I watched all this from a cramped booth overlooking the Bunker's operations room. The IWO booth was an enclosed structure that restricted access from most military staff, even those who occupied the upper command level of the Bunker, allowing entry only to intelligence staff and the U.S. Air Force Sector Controllers – the officers in charge of the command center. The booth contained a variety of communications devices along with a computerized radar console where I could access the specific flight data of all air traffic being shown on the big screen in front of us.

Other staff on this upper level, or dais as the Americans called it, consisted of an Air Force officer weatherman and the Sector Controller on duty, usually a U.S. Air Force Lieutenant Colonel. Also there on the shift and intentionally placed furthest away from our top-secret intelligence booth sat a French military observer and a German military liaison officer, both posted as passive observers for their countries.

The spacious operations room below the command dais consisted of about a hundred personnel on each of the three daily shifts placed on three more levels. Directly below the command dais was the U.S. Army missile command staff level. Below them were the Air Force aircraft control and warning radar controllers, "scope dopes" as they were affectionately called, along with a mixture of German Luftwaffe (air force) troops and civilian German air traffic controllers, also on radarscopes.

While we worked inside this massive concrete box, there was no natural light in the operations center. With only ambient light from the blips and sweeps of radarscopes and radar console buttons and low-wattage desk lamps, the scene resembled a movie theater, including step lights for the stairs on each level. The system's integrated radar input provided a continuous display of the airborne participants in this big-screen production of deterrence and defense called the Cold War – certainly a grander production than anything coming out of Hollywood.

At a cost of countless billions of dollars with a cast of tens of thousands in supporting roles, the eyes and ears of the command center were fixed on and responsive to each movement and maneuver in the dangerous scenario being played out between the member countries of NATO and the Soviet Union-controlled Warsaw Pact countries.

The command bunker was a massive concrete underground complex, consisting of a main control center on four levels that accommodated on-duty personnel, communications gear and more than fifty radarscope consoles. Within the NATO defense command system, it was called Command Bunker Erwin. The Americans who worked there called it the Bunker. (A cutaway view of the Bunker is provided in the Illustrations section at the front of this book.)

The main operations room was almost two hundred and forty feet long from the front display screen to the rear wall behind the command staff. It was more than one hundred and seventy feet wide, and more than eighty feet from the lower floor to the ceiling. To give a sense of the magnitude of the operations center, it was only slightly smaller than the full seating and stage area of the largest indoor theater in the world, the Radio City Music Hall in New York City.

Behind the operations center on three floors was another underground concrete bunker that housed the electrical generators that provided an independent power source for the facility. All of the exterior concrete walls for both bunkers were nearly twelve feet thick and their roofs consisted of steel I-beams covered with more than thirteen feet of reinforced poured concrete. The entire concrete and steel structure was buried beneath a twenty-foot layer of soil and forest growth that provided additional protection and some camouflage.

In an early briefing, I had been told that the Bunker, along with its electrical generator rooms and various support compartments, all encased in concrete and steel, had been constructed as a nuclear-proof facility that sat atop sets of steel springs intended to absorb the shock of a surface blast from a nuclear weapon.

Initially, I was impressed with and comforted by this knowledge. I had been informed that the Bunker would provide a livable environment for several weeks since it was a self-contained facility capable of surviving a direct hit from a medium-yield air burst nuclear attack.

When I had a chance to let this sink in, I realized that it was hardly comforting to know that, in the event of a nuclear exchange over Central Europe, I might live long enough to witness the total destruction of the military and civilian populations in Central Europe and then live a few weeks longer than most of its inhabitants. The prospect of a nuclear conflict being set off provided me with a grim reminder of the necessity to do my job very well and that I had better ensure that I and my fellow workers remained alert and competent in carrying out our assigned tasks.

We were playing a serious game with potentially severe consequences. I understood early on that I had to pay very close attention to everything I was told and that I would have to fully understand and be able to apply all the procedure and planning documents that I had to study. This was all classified information up to top-secret, so there would be no note-taking or crib sheets and I had to know my policies and procedures cold so that I could instantly respond with appropriate actions. Any examination of my knowledge had to be passed at a hundred percent, or the results could be fatal.

By the late summer of 1967, I had become comfortable working without training officer oversight and had been assigned my first solo run, trusted to hold the intelligence watch post on a midnight shift. That shift was eleven p.m. until seven a.m., what I used to call an all-nighter in my college days. I was bit nervous, but fortunately I had been assigned to team up with a very competent and experienced senior officer holding the Sector Controller post during my first watch.

Besides, having achieved a somewhat professional level of all-nighter performance by my senior year in college, I was functioning in my best hours of operation and fully involved with the task to hand.

Having worked only on day shifts during my training period for the past two months, by three a.m. I had become perhaps a bit too relaxed in the middle of my first solo shift and nearly nodded off. Seated in my well-fitted, government-issue swivel office chair, I rescued myself from a self-induced whiplash when I was suddenly roused to attention by the bright warning light above the display screen at the front of the operations center.

This light functioned as an alarm to all those on duty in the Bunker, indicating that a possible border violation had been detected. My immediate reaction was the sudden fear that somehow we were going to experience a significant Soviet intrusion into NATO airspace on my first watch!

I quickly dismissed that thought as I saw the warning light go out. Fortunately, this incident turned out to be a false alarm and the alert was cancelled. It had been induced only by a brief data glitch in the system.

Then, just to make sure everything was under control and that there could be no air traffic mishaps or omitted observations on my shift, I meticulously scanned the giant display screen in front of me that showed all air traffic over West and East Germany and over their neighboring countries. Better to err with an overly cautious attitude than assume that all was well.

The command center screen was unique and the latest development in command post technology that would later be implemented by U.S. forces throughout the world. It provided a forty-foot-by-forty-foot Plexiglas clear acrylic plastic sheet with a projection map that showed the borders of the countries surrounding West Germany.

Still somewhat bleary-eyed and stupefied in this early morning hour, I lit another cigarette to stimulate whatever consciousness I could stir up and then promised myself another cup of the distasteful vending machine coffee provided at the nearby snack room at four a.m. This would help me through the rest of the morning. Nodding off on a watch is bad form and to be avoided on any military post, and particularly when your official post title is Intelligence *Watch* Officer.

The Bunker had been designed to avoid visual detection from the road or from aerial traffic. What had once been a mountain hilltop had been bulldozed away and a large crater had been excavated to accommodate the eighty-foot-deep structure. It was then covered with soil and trees, thereby reconstituting the hilltop and leaving only a mound of soil with a metal entrance door that opened to the two-hundred-foot long tunnel leading to the command operations center.

On my first day, I sensed that I had just passed through the looking glass and that I was about to discover a strange world where I would come to expect nothing but extraordinary things to happen. And so they did!

In fact, the Bunker was accessed from a small, fenced-off parking lot where there were no visible buildings and located a short distance away from a little-used forest road. The exhaust gases of the internal electrical generators were surrounded by a stream of air forced through dissipation heat exchangers, making the Bunker invisible to thermal imaging devices that might search the area.

The facility was well hidden unless one questioned the presence of a parking lot with several personal vehicles bearing U.S. military license plates on a parking lot surrounded by a shady pine and birch forest. It seemed as if someone had been following a perverse obsession to pave paradise and put up a parking lot, or perhaps this was only the result of a misguided attempt by a military engineering unit to conceal the primary military Command Center for Central Europe.

WHAT WE WERE WATCHING

WHILE ATTENDING VARIOUS COURSES IN college and in my independent research, I had studied the military and political history of Europe through its centuries of wars up to and including the Cold War. I had never imagined that I would become a player in this game that had been researched, studied and speculated about by numerous professors of history and political science, and now I had just been thrust into the thick of the conflict, with textbook theorizing brought to life in my daily post functions.

My college studies in political science had given me an overview of the international tensions and the high-risk hornet's nest that was the Cold War, but it certainly had not prepared me for day-to-day participation in carrying out the principles of deterrence and defense as we faced the Iron Curtain in the late 1960s. Among my studies was the popular "Introduction to International Relations" course delivered at Yale by Professor H. Bradford Westerfield.

At the time I took this course, Westerfield was an admitted self-styled "hawk" with his advocacy of an aggressive policy toward the ongoing Vietnam War. He had become well known for shaping the hard-line approach of U.S. foreign policy. His courses had been attended by more than ten thousand students at Yale, including President George W. Bush, Vice President Dick Cheney, Senators John Kerry and Joseph Lieberman during my time at Yale, along with assorted cabinet officers, White House advisers and intelligence officials who have frequently acknowledged his influence on their approach to public policy.

Personally, I found the course tedious and pointless with its dismal and hopeless portrayal of foreign relations for a world in conflict that discouraged me from any hope or interest in international politics. Such topics as Deterrence and Defense, the Sino (Chinese) -Soviet Conflict, the hostile threats of communist leaders, the obvious duplicity of U.S. politicians and the covert influence of international bankers had convinced me that I was not suited for a career in global leadership in foreign affairs or international economics.

After attending three lectures of the course, I had gained a sufficient understanding of Westerfield's views on international affairs. I then determined to merely study the assigned textbooks for the course, along with Westerfield's most recently published textbook, in preparation for the final exam. This was a lesson that I had learned well in college: if I could get inside the head of the professor, I just might anticipate the exam questions or subject of the test and ensure a passing grade. Since this was my early-morning class, I was now able to pursue my interest in Hollywood movies of the 1930s and 1940s that were being shown on late-night TV and also fit in an occasional round of golf at the school's championship golf course. Altogether, this was an enjoyable use of my time that resulted in a satisfactory B grade for the course.

As I became less interested in such subjects, I found that my visits to the college bookstore to acquire course texts often resulted in the purchase of slim volumes of poetry collections from twentieth-century American poets such as T.S. Eliot, e.e. cummings (his preferred non-capitalization), Robert Frost, Hart Crane and even Allen Ginsberg's *Howl* that depicted the destructive forces of materialism and conformity in the twentieth century.

These masters of insight and expression revealed a world of more complex social, moral and philosophical themes than I would ever have encountered in my studies from "authorities" on the subjects of history, politics and economics. The aesthetic messages of these and other poets had subtly reoriented my viewpoint and would influence preferences and actions that would change the course of my life.

Decades later, following the U.S. military and political disaster of Vietnam, Dr. Westerfield modified and softened his earlier stance of uncompromising anti-communism. When I learned that he had recanted his earlier hard-line views, I was reminded of the exasperated comment of "never mind" from comic Gilda Radner's befuddled news reporter Roseanne Roseannadanna on *Saturday Night Live* when she learned that her opinions were based on a complete misunderstanding of the subject. Well, Professor Westerfield, just like Miss Roseannadanna said, "it just goes to show you, it's always something."

What was this underground command center tucked away in the southwestern German mountains looking for? The continuous observation of the giant display screen showed the movement of air traffic across Central Europe and provided a dynamic moment-by-moment view of the European theater of aircraft operations. (An illustration of the SOC III area of operations and facilities is provided in the Illustrations section at the front of this book.)

To my left lay France, Luxembourg and the Netherlands. On the right stood East Germany, Czechoslovakia and Poland. Austria and Switzerland lay to the right and south. And we were located at the center of the defensive shield of West Germany. From my independent studies of German history and also from German literature, I knew well how this had all come about.

Following the defeat of Germany in World War II in 1945, western Germany had been divided into the three Allied Zones of occupation held by the United States, the United Kingdom and France, with the French turning over their southwest zone to the U.S. in 1949.

In accordance with agreements made after World War II in 1945, the Soviet Union occupied the eastern portion of Germany and the Allies occupied western Germany. Also, the U.S., the United Kingdom, and France controlled the western portions of the former capital city of Berlin, while Soviet troops controlled the eastern sector of that city.

The Soviets soon found the situation in Berlin intolerable due to the city's location in the heart of their eastern occupation zone of Germany. In an effort to reunite Berlin through force and intimidation, the Soviets imposed a blockade in 1948 that closed off all land access routes into the city in what was to become known as the Berlin Blockade.

The U.S. and Great Britain responded to the blockade with a continuous flow of cargo aircraft that delivered food, coal, and other necessities into the city until the Soviets removed the blockade in mid-1949.

As a result of those actions and responses, the Iron Curtain had been clearly defined by the Soviets through the construction of fences and walls monitored by armed border guards with armored vehicles and military weapons that enforced limited access to East Germany and Berlin. As relations hardened between the Cold War adversaries, Germany became the primary potential battleground for the onset of World War III and, anticipating that, U.S. troop levels tripled from 1950 to 1953. A quarter million U.S. troops had been stationed in continuous readiness throughout West Germany.

After the blockade, radar stations were strategically placed in West Germany, providing a watchful eye on Soviet bloc air activities and reporting on any violations of West German air space. Sector Operations Center III was the primary unit charged with appropriate response to and defense from any hostile Warsaw Pact aerial encroachment.

The SOC in the Bunker also had the responsibility of monitoring the commerce and air traffic to and from Berlin within its three air access corridors, ensuring that aircraft remained on course and within certain restrictions agreed to with the Soviets following the Berlin Blockade and Airlift. According to those agreements, each air corridor was limited to a twenty-mile width, and aircraft were required to fly at a maximum height of ten thousand feet. The commercial pilots had to be highly proficient and attentive to stay within these limits.

Slight deviations outside the corridors resulted in immediate Soviet jet fighter interceptor response to any errant aircraft. Occasionally, we would observe Soviet fighter aircraft taking off and conducting mock intercepts on civilian aircraft in the corridors, but they would keep their distance and return to their bases after getting our attention and giving the civilian pilots a scare.

Each of these mock intercepts had been met with generally calm reactions from all personnel in the Bunker.

It was, after all, one of the primary missions of the Bunker to defend against such aggression and to ensure that Berlin was not cut off from traffic to and from the west. All hands, even the weatherman, were practiced in ensuring timely and effective response in the event of an actual attack on aircraft in the corridors. And, of course, any U.S. Air Force aircraft response would be directed by the Sector Controller with the advice of the Intelligence Watch Officer.

To back up its defense of West Germany, the SOC III command staff had at its disposal three tactical air defense fighter aircraft squadrons, along with command control of the U.S. Army Nike Hercules missile units and Hawk anti-aircraft missile units. Even after the French withdrawal of missile forces stationed in Germany in 1966, the integrated surface-to-air missile defense system consisted of seven U.S. Army Nike Hercules battalions and nine U.S. Army Hawk battalions, forming a broad missile defense shield in southwestern Germany in anticipation of any Soviet missile or aircraft attacks. Altogether, a formidable arsenal poised just outside the Iron Curtain.

The Bunker was equipped with the 412L radar data integration system, a very sophisticated piece of electronic hardware for the 1960s. General Electric had developed this system for the U.S. Air Force to compile data and present it on radarscopes. This single comprehensive information center allowed operators to track, assign, identify, or target any airborne object.

This was the real-life computer combat system that would later become the model for the video games that I would watch my sons and grandsons play on their game consoles and computers. I would also see the display of integrated defense systems shown in films like *War Games* that would thrill sci-fi and action movie audiences.

Within the 412L system, all radar units had a direct connection to SOC III in the Bunker which was able to communicate with practically any military unit using the microwave repeater station towers that linked military facilities throughout Europe and beyond to other line-of-site command stations across the NATO member countries. From our underground lair, we had "magic in our eyes" and we could "see for miles and miles and miles."

The three fighter interceptor squadrons under SOC III control were stationed at Hahn, Bitburg and Ramstein air bases, all U.S. Air Force bases in southwestern Germany. These fighter squadrons flew our aircraft intercepts in F-102 Delta Dagger jet aircraft. Each squadron had two or four of the Delta Daggers in a "Zulu Alert" hangar, where they were kept ready to take off within a few minutes of receiving a Zulu scramble order from us.

The pilots and their ground crews were well-practiced in scrambling, a military term used to describe quickly getting aircraft airborne to react to a threat, usually to intercept hostile aircraft or missiles. Pilots and ground-based crews lived in the two-story Zulu hangar while on Zulu Alert assignment. During a scramble, the crew would slide down a fireman's pole from its second-floor living quarters to the aircraft in the hangar.

The F-102s were able to get airborne within three to five minutes of receiving the initial alarm from the SOC and they could attain a forty-thousand-foot altitude in less than five minutes after takeoff. They were able to be equipped with conventional or nuclear anti-aircraft missiles. Additional jet fighters were maintained on standby alert at each air base, if needed in a major conflict.

All Hawk surface-to-air missile battalions and all Nike Hercules battalions with four units each and their associated mission control centers were connected for tactical control within the integrated network under SOC III. This enabled the Sector Operations Center to provide early warning data from the entire NATO early warning system and ensure that all missile forces would respond to orders issued from the SOC to protect friendly aircraft or blow away entire formations of high-altitude supersonic targets.

With seven nuclear- and conventional-capable Nike Hercules units and three nuclear- and conventional-ready tactical aircraft squadrons of F-102s, along with nine Hawk anti-aircraft missile units, SOC III controlled the largest and most intimidating concentration of weapons on alert status outside the continental U.S. in the 1960s.

Out of college for about a year, it seemed that I had dropped down the rabbit hole with so many remarkable things happening and I had begun to think that very few things indeed were really impossible. I was now an essential member of the command team in control of a formidable military force. How could that have happened?

WHAT A TANGLED WEB WE WOVE

MY UNANTICIPATED SERVICE IN THE military in Germany was the result of a series of events that commenced in early 1964, when the South Vietnamese Navy began conducting a covert series of U.S.-backed commando attacks and intelligence-gathering missions along the North Vietnamese coast that lies on the Gulf of Tonkin.

The Gulf is the northwest arm of the South China Sea and is only about three hundred miles long and one hundred and fifty miles wide. It is a shallow ocean inlet at a depth of less than two hundred feet. As an arm of that sea, it is a very small segment. There are some freshwater lakes with a comparable surface area such as Lake Michigan which is three to four times as deep as the Gulf of Tonkin.

These attacks were part of Operations Plan 34A and were designed to prevent the North Vietnamese communist forces from overcoming the military forces of South Vietnam being supported by the U.S.

The Plan's activities were conceived and overseen by the U.S. Department of Defense, with support from the

Central Intelligence Agency, and it was carried out by the South Vietnamese Navy. Plan 34A was focused on offshore assaults against North Vietnamese coastal installations. These attacks had resulted in very limited success with numerous South Vietnamese raiders being captured and the raiding units frequently suffering heavy casualties.

In July 1964, Lieutenant General William Westmoreland, commander of the U.S. Military Assistance Command in Vietnam (the primary U.S. presence in the area), shifted the operation's tactics to more effective commando attacks on land-to-shore bombardments using mortars, rockets, and recoilless rifles that fired artillery shells from the South Vietnamese patrol boats. These attacks were using heavier artillery that had now taken the conflict into its next level of escalation.

Meanwhile, the U.S. Navy had been conducting occasional reconnaissance and signals intelligence-gathering missions further offshore in the Gulf of Tonkin. Signals intelligence (SIGINT) is accomplished through the interception of signals, whether communications between people, communications intelligence (COMINT), or from electronic signals not directly used in communication.

U.S. Navy destroyers carried out these passive intelligence-gathering patrols in the Gulf of Tonkin. After the missions that had been deployed in December 1962 and April of the next year, patrols were scheduled for 1964 in the vicinity of the South Vietnamese raids. In fact, one of the primary missions of the patrols was to gather information from communications intercepts that would provide intelligence about North Vietnamese troop deployments, planning and strategies for use by the South Vietnamese raiders.

A top-secret document declassified in 2005 revealed that the standing orders to these intelligence-gathering patrols was to, "Locate and identify all coastal radar transmitters, note all navigation aids along the Democratic Republic of Vietnam's [North Vietnam's] coastline, and monitor the Vietnamese junk fleet for a possible connection to North Vietnam/Viet Cong maritime supply and infiltration routes."

United States forces were now getting deeply involved in this dangerous armed conflict. The South Vietnamese had been conducting OPLAN 34A raids and the U.S. Navy's heavily armed intelligence-gathering destroyers could only be perceived by the North Vietnamese as being part of a U.S. collaborative effort with South Vietnam against North Vietnamese targets.

On 2 August 1964, the destroyer USS *Maddox* was cruising in international waters twenty-eight miles off the coast of North Vietnam, performing its signals intelligence patrol, when it encountered three North Vietnamese torpedo boats. The *Maddox* was specially equipped with a communications intercept van on board that housed seventeen signals intelligence specialists. The ship was primarily a well-fortified intelligence-gathering facility equipped with the latest communications intercept technology.

The *Maddox* had been present during earlier South Vietnamese naval attacks against North Vietnamese military targets in its role of providing intelligence information in support of the raiders. Having been associated with earlier attacks on North Vietnamese facilities, the *Maddox* became a likely target for the three North Vietnamese Navy motor torpedo boats patrolling in the area.

Each torpedo boat was sixty-six-feet long with an aluminum hull, comparable to the size of a modern sport fishing boat. These boats were hardly a match for the steel-hulled U.S. Navy destroyer that was forty feet wide and longer than an American football field.

In the early hours of August 2, the *Maddox* communications technicians intercepted signal reports of North Vietnamese vessels getting underway, with the possible intent of attacking the destroyer. The commander of the U.S. Navy 7th Fleet group of destroyers, Captain John J. Herrick, was on board the *Maddox*. He ordered the vessel out to sea away from the Gulf which would have avoided a confrontation.

Then he reversed his orders, turning the *Maddox* back toward the coast, openly and deliberately antagonizing the potential attackers and forcing a confrontation. Weather conditions were clear and seas were calm and the destroyer easily detected the three North Vietnamese patrol boats approaching from the west. Aware of the North Vietnamese boats' intended course of action from the earlier signals intelligence message, Herrick ordered the *Maddox*'s captain to have gun crews fire upon the torpedo boats if they came within ten thousand yards, nearly six miles away. When they did come that close, the American sailors fired three rounds to warn off the North Vietnamese patrol boats.

Maximum effective weapon range for the torpedo boats was one thousand yards, but *Maddox*'s five-inch guns had a range of eighteen thousand yards. The three hundred and thirty-six *Maddox* crew members on a vessel of two thousand tons of water displacement was now attacking three torpedo boats, each with a maximum of twelve crew and twenty tons of water displacement.

The *Maddox* had six five-inch guns, twenty-three anti-aircraft guns, ten torpedo tubes, and six depth-charge projectors. This array of weaponry was up against three torpedo boats, each with two seventeen-inch torpedoes and two 14.5-millimeter machine guns. The North Vietnamese boats presented hardly a contest and barely a threat to the fully armed U.S. Navy destroyer.

As the torpedo boats continued their attack, one boat attempted to run alongside the *Maddox* for a side shot, while the remaining two boats continued their stern chase. The two chasers fired first but, due to the *Maddox*'s heavy fire of five-inch shells, the torpedo boats were forced to discharge their torpedoes from too great a distance and all four underwater missiles missed their marks.

The lead boat also fired its torpedoes without effect when the *Maddox* altered its course to avoid the torpedoes, which were observed passing on its starboard side. The lead patrol boat dueled with the *Maddox*'s five-inch guns using its twin 14.5-millimeter armor-piercing machine gun, achieving a single hit on the destroyer.

Soon after the engagement began, four supersonic, carrier-based jet aircraft F-8 Crusaders arrived from an aircraft carrier in the region, the USS *Ticonderoga*, and attacked the three torpedo boats. In what was claimed to be a sea battle, the combination of fire from the *Maddox* which expended two-hundred and eighty five-inch shells along with strafing from the four U.S. Navy supersonic fighter aircraft, severely damaged all three boats and forced them to retreat to the bases from which they had come.

Several North Vietnamese Navy sailors were wounded and four were killed. No U.S. sailors were killed or wounded, and the *Maddox* did not sustain significant damage, just the lone machine-gun bullet. One of the four F-8 Crusader fighter aircraft sustained some 14.5 mm machine gunfire hits, losing a large portion of its left wing but it managed to return to the *Ticonderoga*.

This was the actual unreported brief skirmish that occurred before the Gulf of Tonkin "incident" that was later used to justify a declaration of war based on the fabricated incident that took place two days later.

It was likely that the "sensitive compartmented information" classified nature of the signals intelligence activities being conducted by the *Maddox* at the time would have prevented any immediate disclosure of this minor incident. So, this actual combat action between a U.S. Navy destroyer and four Navy aircraft against three North Vietnamese patrol boats was never confirmed until four decades later.

The next day, the *Maddox* resumed its patrol. To demonstrate American resolve and the right to navigate in international waters, traditionally regarded as "saber-rattling," U.S. President Lyndon Baines Johnson ordered the destroyer USS *Turner Joy* to join the *Maddox* on patrol off the North Vietnamese coast. Now, two destroyers and an aircraft carrier had been deployed to the Gulf of Tonkin in search of real or imagined trouble.

That night, the South Vietnamese staged more raids with three patrol craft attacking a security garrison at the mouth of a major river and a radar site in North Vietnam. They fired seven hundred and seventy rounds of high-explosive munitions at the targets. North Vietnamese coastal installations had now been attacked four separate times in five days. The war between South and North Vietnam was intensifying.

WHAT DIDN'T HAPPEN ACTUALLY

WHAT REPORTEDLY OCCURRED TWO DAYS later in the Gulf of Tonkin on August 4 and the actions taken by Washington officials had been cloaked in deception and confusion until 2005 when the National Security Agency revealed what actually happened through its release of two hundred now-declassified documents. More than one hundred and forty of these documents had been classified as top-secret.

A historical study released in that documentation concluded that the *Maddox* had engaged the North Vietnamese Navy on August 2, but that "there had been no North Vietnamese naval vessels present during the incident of August 4." That deserves to be repeated, "There had been no North Vietnamese naval vessels present during the incident of August 4," the purported date of the Gulf of Tonkin incident, the cause for a declaration of war.

After decades of cover-up, this historical study revealed the "incident" to have been a fraud perpetrated on the people of America and the world. From these declassified documents we now know that high government officials, including Secretary of Defense Robert McNamara and President Lyndon B. Johnson, had distorted facts and deceived the American public about events that led to the U.S. commitment to a full-scale war in Vietnam. This was how it was done.

The National Security Agency had claimed that a Second Gulf of Tonkin incident occurred on August 4, 1964, as another sea battle, but instead evidence was found of what had later been referred to as "Tonkin Ghosts" (misinterpreted radar images) without any presence of actual North Vietnamese torpedo boats.

In the 2003 documentary *The Fog of War*, former Secretary of Defense Robert McNamara admitted that the August 2 USS *Maddox* minor attack had happened but with no Defense Department response, and that the August 4 Gulf of Tonkin attack had never happened actually.

On the morning of August 4, U.S. intelligence intercepted a report indicating that the North Vietnamese communists intended to conduct offensive maritime operations in the Gulf of Tonkin. In contrast to the clear weather conditions two days earlier, thunderstorms and rainsqualls reduced visibility and increased wave heights to six feet. In addition to the difficult radar and sonar detection conditions, the *Maddox*'s long-range air-search radar and the *Turner Joy*'s fire-control radar were both inoperative. The two ships were moved out to sea to give themselves maneuvering space in case of an attack.

Despite limited visibility and high wave conditions, the *Maddox* reported in the early evening that it was tracking unidentified vessels. Although the U.S. destroyers were operating more than a hundred miles from the North Vietnamese coastline, the approaching vessels seemed to come at the ships from multiple directions, according to reports from the crew on board. Some "attacking" vessels seemed to come from the northeast, others from the southwest. Still other targets appeared from the east, mimicking attacking profiles of torpedo boats, according to crew reports. Targets would disappear and then new targets would appear from the opposite compass direction.

Over the next three hours, the two destroyers repeatedly maneuvered at high speeds to evade the perceived enemy boat attacks. The destroyers reported automatic-weapons fire; more than twenty torpedo attacks; sightings of torpedo wakes, enemy cockpit lights, and searchlight illuminations; and numerous radar and surface contacts. By the time the destroyers broke off their "counterattack," they had fired two hundred and forty-nine five-inch shells, one hundred and twenty-three three-inch shells, and four or five depth charges.

Navy pilot Commander James Bond Stockdale got permission to launch a solo flight from the nearby USS *Ticonderoga* to assess the scene. He flew over the "battle" site for more than ninety minutes and made runs parallel to the course of the two U.S. destroyers at an altitude below two thousand feet, searching for the enemy vessels. He reported later, "I had the best seat in the house to watch that event and our destroyers were just shooting at phantom targets – there were no PT boats there … there was nothing there but black water and American firepower."

Destroyer fleet commander Captain Herrick also began to have doubts about the attack. As the battle continued, he realized the "attacks" were actually the results of "overeager sonar operators" and poor equipment performance. The *Turner Joy* had not detected any incoming torpedoes during the entire encounter, and Herrick determined that the *Maddox*'s operators were probably hearing the ship's propellers reflecting off their own rudders during sharp turns. The destroyer's main artillery director was never able to lock onto any targets because, as the operator surmised, the radar was detecting the stormy sea's wave tops.

Hours after the so-called "attacks" had occurred, Herrick queried his crew and reviewed the preceding events. He sent a highest priority message that was received in Washington on August 4, declaring his doubts: "Review of action makes many reported contacts and torpedoes fired appear doubtful. Freak weather effects on radar and overeager sonar men may have accounted for many reports. No actual visual sightings by *Maddox*. Suggest complete evaluation before any further action taken."

Messages declassified in 2005 along with recently released audiotapes from the Lyndon Baines Johnson Library reveal confusion among the leadership in Washington, as well. Calls between the Joint Chiefs of Staff; the National Military Command Center; headquarters of the Commander in Chief, Pacific; and Secretary of Defense McNamara were frequently exchanged during the phantom battle. Since Vietnam was twelve hours ahead of Washington time, the "attacks" in the evening of August 4 were being monitored in Washington in the late morning of that date. Herrick sent another report in which he changed his previous story:

"Certain that original ambush was bonafide. Details of action following present a confusing picture. Have interviewed witnesses who made positive visual sightings of cockpit lights or similar passing near *Maddox*. Several reported torpedoes were probably boats themselves which were observed to make several close passes on *Maddox*. Own ship screw noises on rudders may have accounted for some. At present cannot even estimate number of boats involved. *Turner Joy* reports two torpedoes passed near her."

This was an obvious attempt to explain a series of chaotic events amid disorderly and incompetent responses to them that had resulted in alarming reports of some imagined enemy activity. In military terminology, this should have been acknowledged as yet another SNAFU (Situation Normal, All Fouled Up, in its polite form), but there was a political advantage to be gained here.

McNamara phoned Admiral Ulysses S. Grant Sharp, commander of the U.S. Pacific Command, to talk it over and asked, "Was there a possibility that there had been no attack?" Sharp admitted that there was a "slight possibility" because of freak radar echoes, inexperienced sonar operators and no visual sightings of torpedo wakes. The admiral added that he was trying to get more information and recommended placing on hold any order for a retaliatory strike against North Vietnam until "we have a definite indication of what happened."

An unconfirmed intercepted message from one of the North Vietnamese patrol boats seemed to substantiate the belief that an attack had occurred, stating that the patrol boat had, "Shot down two planes in the battle area. We sacrificed two comrades but all the rest are okay. The enemy ship could also have been damaged." In Washington, Air Force General David Burchinal, the director of the Joint Chiefs of Staff, determined that the new communications intercept "pins it down better than anything so far." However, there had been no report of any U.S. aircraft being shot down or shot at, and not a single report of munitions damage to any U.S. vessels.

McNamara had somehow determined that this boastful, unsubstantiated report from a third-world navy patrol boat crew claiming to be under attack from two well-armed U.S. Navy destroyers, coupled with Admiral Sharp's belief that the attack was "possibly" authentic, was now seen to be conclusive proof of hostile acts of war.

When President Johnson asked during an August 4 meeting of the National Security Council, "Do they want a war by attacking our ships in the middle of the Gulf of Tonkin?" CIA Director John McCone answered, "No, the North Vietnamese are reacting defensively to our attacks on their offshore islands ... the attack is a signal to us that the North Vietnamese have the will and determination to continue the war."

Nevertheless, that evening President Johnson appeared on national television and announced his intent to retaliate against North Vietnamese targets: "Repeated acts of violence against the armed forces of the United States must be met not only with alert defense, but with positive reply. The reply is being given as I speak to you tonight." And retaliate they did, with the first actual U.S. Navy air strike against a strategic military target in North Vietnam.

Aboard the U.S. Navy aircraft carrier *Ticonderoga*, Commander Stockdale had been ordered to prepare the launch of an air strike against North Vietnamese targets in response to their "attacks" of the previous evening. Stockdale had no doubt about what had happened. Years later, he would reveal that, "We were about to launch a war under false pretenses, in the face of the on-scene military commander's advice to the contrary."

Despite his reservations, Stockdale led a strike of eighteen aircraft against an oil storage facility at Vinh, North Vietnam, located just inland from where the alleged attacks on the *Maddox* and *Turner Joy* had supposedly occurred. The raid was very successful, with the oil storage depot completely destroyed and thirty-three of the thirty-five vessels at the depot hit by the air strikes. Two of the

American aircraft were shot down with one pilot killed and another captured.

Since regretted actions or behavior often have a way of ending up in negative consequences, someone knowingly carrying out orders to launch an "act of war under false pretenses" just might incur an unanticipated reversal of fortune. On his next deployment over North Vietnam, Commander Stockdale was shot down and held as a prisoner of war for seven years in North Vietnam at the infamous "Hanoi Hilton." Yes, what goes around does come around.

At this time in my life in 1964, I had no concern about air strikes in distant Southeast Asia while I was working the final weeks on my summer job and getting ready to return to college where I would be running the school's Student Furniture Agency, selling used furniture from departing seniors to incoming freshmen to help pay for my tuition. It had not occurred to me that American political deceptions would interrupt the course of my life in the near future.

Two days later, after the oil depot attack, on August 7, the United States Congress, with only two dissenting votes, approved the Gulf of Tonkin Resolution, signed into law by President Johnson soon thereafter. Requested by Johnson, the resolution authorized the chief executive to, "take all necessary measures to repel any armed attack against the forces of the United States and to prevent further aggression." On hearing of the authorization's passage by both houses of Congress, the delighted President remarked in his characteristic "good-old-boy" style that the resolution "was like Grandma's nightshirt. It covers everything."

Johnson himself apparently had his own doubts about what happened in the Gulf on August 4. A few days after the Gulf of Tonkin Resolution was passed, he was heard to comment privately, "Hell, those damn stupid sailors were just shooting at flying fish."

The truth of what occurred was now irrelevant, as it had just provided Johnson with the legal justification for deploying U.S. conventional forces and the commencement of open warfare against North Vietnam. The resolution made it possible to not require approval or oversight of military force by Congress. In essence, the system of checks and balances fundamental to the U.S. Constitution had been suspended.

A few months later, during his campaign for election in November 1964, Lyndon Johnson told audiences at campaign stops that some American leaders wanted to send more troops to Vietnam, but he did not agree, and he stressed that, "We are not about to send American boys nine or ten thousand miles away to do what Asian boys ought to do for themselves."

This was promised while Johnson knew that his senior commanders at the Pentagon were recommending that the U.S. should use Air Force bombers to assist South Vietnamese troops, that trails leading into North Vietnam – where most of the insurgents were trained and supplied – should be bombed and that an American air base, guarded by U.S. troops, should be built near the South Vietnamese capitol of Saigon.

Johnson assured all congressmen and the American public that he hoped to be able to negotiate a settlement that would prevent this, but he had already covertly given permission for American military planners to prepare for bombing missions in Vietnam as needed.

Portraying his Republican opponent Barry Goldwater as an extreme proponent for aggressive military action who would escalate the conflict in Vietnam, and with the assistance of national media promoting that unpopular course of action if Goldwater became President, Johnson was able to win over the Democrats along with the moderate and liberal Republicans who had been reluctant to escalate the conflict in Vietnam. They would soon be in for a surprise.

On November 3, 1964, three months after the Gulf of Tonkin Resolution, Lyndon B. Johnson won the presidential election in the greatest landslide victory since 1820 when he received four hundred and eighty-six electoral college votes to the fifty-two obtained by his Republican opponent, Barry Goldwater.

Johnson had achieved his objective: he was no longer merely the inheritor of the throne left vacant a year earlier by the assassination of President John F. Kennedy. He was now the chosen leader of the free world, with a strong mandate to carry out his worldview as ultimately expressed in his "Great Society" government welfare programs.

Johnson and his cohorts, including Robert McNamara and surely many others who had worked in the shadows, had accomplished a sweeping victory that would enable his administration to carry on a hopeless, misguided war with little or no interference from Congress. Lies and deceptions had deeply entangled the United States in a conflict that proved to be destructive to countless lives in Vietnam and America.

After winning the presidential election, Johnson was aware that he might regret his perceived "promise" to keep "American boys" out of Asia. He assured Congressional supporters and advisors that if he had to commit more troops to Vietnam that he would not call up reserve units or National Guard units, for that would probably disrupt the economy and his plans for domestic legislation, and also cost him support from congressmen.

He determined that he would merely rely on involuntarily drafted soldiers by doubling the number of draft orders, ultimately resulting in more than two million young American men being conscripted into service between 1964 and 1973, a nine-year period in what is now known as the Vietnam Era.

Thus commenced an awareness of betrayal and distrust among the youth of America, with tuneful anthems lamenting that "there's something happening here, but what it is ain't exactly clear." This was starting to seem like something that was going to have a profound impact on my life.

* * *

As a footnote to what has recently been revealed about the events that embroiled the U.S. in one of its longest wars, former Secretary of Defense Robert McNamara's memoir published in 1995 portrayed an account and analysis of the Vietnam War in which he, "concluded well before leaving the Pentagon that the war was futile," but he did not share that insight publicly until late in life. Twenty years after the final withdrawal of American military forces from Vietnam, McNamara took a stand against his own conduct of the war as Secretary of Defense, confessing in the memoir that it was "wrong, terribly wrong."

In the video documentary, *The Fog of War*, released in 2003, McNamara admitted that the Vietnam War was the result of the catastrophic failure of American and Vietnamese leaderships to understand each other's intentions. The North Vietnamese were fighting an anti-colonial war of independence waged against the French since 1945 until the French defeat in 1954, and the United States believed it was fighting the Cold War.

But the United States had no intention of colonizing Vietnam or even exerting control in Southeast Asia comparable to what the Soviet Union had imposed on Eastern European countries. And Vietnam actually viewed communist China largely as another threat, not as an ally in the global war against capitalism.

When McNamara visited Vietnam as part of the documentary, he asked his former counterpart in North Vietnam about Chinese support for North Vietnam. His counterpart asked if McNamara had ever read a history textbook, because it was well known that China and Vietnam had been fighting each other for a thousand years.

BIG WIND FROM WASHINGTON

IN THE MONTHS AFTER THE Gulf of Tonkin Resolution, President Johnson rapidly increased the U.S. military presence to escalate the war in South Vietnam, with nearly two hundred thousand troops stationed there by the end of 1965. During the next four years, the Selective Service would induct an average of about three hundred thousand young men annually.

America was very much at war. The expanded draft would require the commitment of hundreds of thousands, and finally more than two million American young men to forego their life plans and dreams. Eventually, nearly sixty thousand of those men would lay down their lives to do battle against the perceived threat of communism in Southeast Asia.

I recall viewing President Lyndon Johnson on television, putting on that sincere and sorrowful public face he would often adopt, lamenting his responsibility, "to send the flower of our youth, our finest young men, into battle" stating that he knew "how their mothers weep and how their families sorrow." But, he explained, America had "no choice" and his actions were necessitated by the North Vietnamese and Communist Chinese quest to "conquer the South, to defeat American power, and to extend the Asiatic dominion of Communism.… An Asia so threatened by Communist domination would certainly imperil the security of the United States itself." Johnson was not beyond referring to an "Asian invasion" thereby invoking the old specter of a "Yellow Peril" wherein the peoples of East Asia had been conceived to pose great danger to the Western world.

Having heard this, I had to consider if I was prepared to commit my life to a war against the spread of communism. As part of my studies of history, politics and economics, I had evaluated communism as yet another in the long line of political philosophies that had resulted in cruel oppression and crimes against humanity only useful to those seeking power over others.

Communism had already shown that it was ultimately destructive to creativity, prosperity and personal liberty. Because it could never really encourage willing contribution from the members of its society, it would most likely implode on itself. The actual problem was that aggressive attempts at territorial expansion by communist countries could certainly impede the real growth and progress of mankind. Not a political system to be supported, but it was certainly not worth pursuing this distraction with the wasting of lives expended while seeking to destroy it.

In my senior year of college in 1966, the military draft was something every male between the age of eighteen and twenty-six thought about as an impending threat to his future. Troop levels in Vietnam were at roughly one hundred and eighty thousand at this point, and by the end of 1968 there would be half a million Americans committed to the war. So, like many other young men in college in those times, my classmates and I were troubled by the prospect of the draft and how to avoid it.

It was around this time that I began to experience occasional nausea and mild indigestion that I suspected were indications of potentially draft-deferring ulcers. After a trip to the school infirmary, I was ordered to undergo a barium swallow test with X-rays that would highlight my esophagus, stomach and small intestine. This uncomfortable procedure consisted of ingesting chalky liquid containing barium that highlighted the areas where ulcers sometimes occur.

As it turned out, I had no ulcers and was given a "clean bill of health," determined by the doctor to be "fit as a fiddle" and some other hackneyed positive health attributes that would classify me as "1-A, eligible for military service." I would have to rely on my usual good fortune to carry me through this one.

Most of the allowed exemptions from induction into military service had been reported in the news media. These were usually only spoken of in quiet conversations with those among us who might be seeking solutions to the draft, as if talking about this was somehow conspiratorial, or in some way breaking the law, or at least unpatriotic. My personal concern was that I did not wish to kill anyone or be killed; but when ordered, I was willing to serve my country and defend it from external aggression. In its simplicity, I probably had been most directly influenced by the Boy Scouts Oath, in which I had for many years repeatedly pledged that I would "do my best to do my duty to God and my Country," being a good citizen, obeying the laws, working to make it a stronger nation, and defending my country and its principles – a likely candidate for the military.

I had suspected that the Vietnam conflict was a manufactured distraction away from the long-threatened and overwhelming prospect of nuclear warfare that had been building up between the U.S. and the Soviet Union for almost two decades. As one of the elements within the principle of deterrence of atomic warfare through "mutually assured destruction" proposed by Secretary of Defense Robert McNamara, the conflict in Southeast Asia had provided what he called a "smaller proxy war" serving as a release of tensions that would draw away from a direct full-scale nuclear conflict between the U.S. and the Soviet Union.

The U.S. system of conscription prompted many young men to volunteer for the armed forces that gave a semblance of choice as to what branch of the military in which to serve. Among those of draft age it was known that if one were inducted into the Army or the Marines, it most likely would lead to a tour of duty in the Vietnam battle zone.

In reviewing the military options that would be most suitable, I determined that service in the Coast Guard or the Peace Corps did not seem to involve the prospect of battle or extreme danger, just an inconvenience. The Navy had most of its bases away from battle areas across the world, so chances were good that Navy assignments would keep one out of harm's way. Even on duty in Southeast Asia, Navy servicemen were usually well protected within steel-clad war vessels that kept their distance from battlefields. And Air Force personnel were either above it all as pilots or protected on air bases, well defended alongside their multimillion-dollar aircraft. These were the only apparent safe choices.

While many young Americans did support the war at first, others saw the draft as a death sentence, being sent to fight in a war for a cause they did not understand or care about. As American troop levels in Vietnam shot upward, more young men of draft age sought to avoid or delay their military service, and there were some legal ways to do that. Some sought refuge in college deferments, continuing their educations into graduate school programs. Those who were married with children or were needed at home to support their families usually obtained deferments.

Men with physical or mental problems were quickly exempted. Yes, flat feet and hearing voices in one's head could merit a deferment. And such tuneful pleas of the time claiming to be "allergic to flowers and bugs, and addicted to a thousand drugs" were heard around draft board centers across the nation.

In the beginning of the war, names of all American men of draft age were collected by the Selective Service System. When someone's name was selected, he had to report to his local draft board, which had enormous power to decide who had to go and who would stay. Consequently, draft board members were often placed under pressure from their families, relatives and friends to exempt potential draftees.

The politically connected often sought refuge in the National Guard, generally enjoying a non-combatant service activity. We referred to them as "the weekend warriors," at the time. Others intentionally failed aptitude tests or otherwise presented undesirable traits.

When a musician friend was called in for his physical exam, he showed up in a borrowed pair of his wife's briefest panties, adopted an effeminate tone of voice and received an instant deferment. Thousands who were less creative fled to Canada and some went south to Mexico. An increasing number engaged in direct resistance, engaging in protest actions such as burning draft cards and marching on government facilities.

In the early stages of the war, those who avoided the draft were derogatorily referred as "draft dodgers," a term made popular during the Vietnam War. In the beginning, many people looked at draft-dodgers as being "cowards." I must confess that initially I viewed their reluctance to serve as an act of disloyalty to our country.

As American casualties escalated, the conflict in Vietnam became increasingly unpopular. Greater numbers of people got involved in the anti-war movement and supported these draft-dodgers, now regarding those who opted to serve in the military with contempt.

In 1966, the year I completed my college education, the United States had ordered more than three hundred and eighty-two thousand young men into compulsory military service, the highest annual number since 1953 at the height of the Korean War.

At my senior class graduation at Yale College in June, 1966, the President of Yale, Kingman Brewster, gave a solemn and earnest address to the new graduates, stating, "There is no greater challenge than to have someone relying upon you; no greater satisfaction than to vindicate his expectation." Little did I realize in the haze of the morning of our graduation following a celebratory night of drinking with some of my fellow graduates how soon I would be challenged and relied upon in my duty to my country.

Two days after my graduation ceremony, a single envelope addressed to me arrived at my parents' mailbox. It was from the local office of the Selective Service System. Some young men were rewarded with cars at graduation, but there was another, bigger surprise in store for me.

In that envelope was a half sheet of paper that boldly declared, "ORDER TO REPORT FOR ARMED FORCES PHYSICAL EXAMINATION." And it demanded that,

"You are hereby ordered to present yourself for Armed Forces Physical Examination to the Local Board named above by reporting at…" then giving the address, date and time of day for the ordered appointment. All very direct with no escape clause to be found.

In the excitement of graduating from life as a student along with a reliance on my usual ability to avoid impending disasters, I had put off any planning to avoid the draft. I now had less than a month to come up with a tolerable solution. Through some connections at the state political level, my father was able to get the local draft board to delay my physical examination and immediate induction for several weeks.

Now, I was getting mildly panicked. I called the local Navy recruiter and was told that they had so many officer applicants that they were arbitrarily denying the applications from anyone with less than twenty-twenty vision. I then called the Coast Guard and was abruptly informed that no officer candidates were being accepted at this time.

As a last resort, I called my school friend Bill who lived in Washington, D.C. I remembered that he had mentioned that his father had been a four-star general in the Air Force. I explained my circumstance to Bill and he immediately called out to his father across their living room. I was able to hear the general reply, "Tell him to join the Air Force as an enlisted man and I'll see to it that he gets into Officer Training School."

Bill relayed that message to me, and I was very relieved. As an Air Force officer I imagined that I would be able to live well during my four years of service, likely in a non-combatant role outside an area of conflict. There was now some hope that I might not become cannon fodder in the misguided and hopeless war in Southeast Asia. I just might achieve my goal of not being killed or having to kill others in an unjust conflict.

The next day, I visited the local Air Force recruiter's office and filled out my enlistment forms. Among the many requests for data, I was being asked for the type of work I would like and where I would like to serve. This was getting interesting. There was a long list of "specialties" to choose from, all those functions that one might expect in a technological field such as aircraft maintenance and air combat support. I would have preferred Advertising as a job preference and an assignment based in New York City, but that was not on the list of choices for a country at war.

So, I selected Intelligence for a job preference, keeping in mind there were probably not a lot of bullets flying around a person analyzing data in a secure, out-of-the-way office. Then, since I had studied the German language for five years and had excelled at it, I naturally chose Germany, entertaining visions of green hills that were alive with the sound of music. I know, that was in Austria; but they spoke German there, too, so it was still an attractive prospect. Any port in a storm, and all along the watchtower, the "winds had begun to howl."

After six weeks of enlisted training and ten weeks of officer training where I achieved the second-highest ranking in my Officer Trainee class, I was shipped off to Air Intelligence School at Lowry Air Force Base in Denver, Colorado. At Lowry, I completed twenty-eight weeks of intelligence training in a wide variety of military subjects that provided necessary instruction for those deploying and defending aircraft and air facilities. All of the data studied was interesting, but most of it informed me only too well as to the methods and tactics of human conflict. I was now in military service in a world engaged in perpetual warfare, at this time in Vietnam, and in the state of continuous geopolitical tension that followed World War II, otherwise known as the Cold War.

Upon graduation, I received assignment orders as an Intelligence Watch Officer at an obscure U.S. Air Force headquarters detachment located in Birkenfeld, Germany. And that's how I ended up eighty feet underground at the NATO command operations center in the Börfink Bunker.

IN THE LINE OF DUTY

AS AN INTELLIGENCE WATCH OFFICER (IWO), the basic description of my duties was outlined in my first Officer Effectiveness Report submitted in late 1967:

"DUTIES: Assesses the active air situation in the Soviet/Satellite forward area, Buffer Zone, Corridors and Air Defense Identification Zone; advises the Sector Controller and the USAFE Indications Center of developments of a threat to Western Europe, reports deviations from the normal air situation, evaluates electronic counter-measures (ECM) reports, compiles a daily and weekly intelligence summary, briefs the Commander and Battle Staff on Soviet/Satellite activities, capabilities and intentions, monitors special interest flights and performs other classified duties not describable herein. ADDITIONAL DUTY: Emergency Actions Officer."

This was reported by my senior, Captain Tony Zilinsky, Officer In Charge, Detachment 6, Special Activities Squadron, a unit within the 17th Air Force that ran the Allied Sector Operations Center III at the

Börfink Bunker. Unlike the Army, the Air Force frequently established organizations that acted as a function with people assigned but no other military formalities, such as staff meetings or unit briefings. SOC III was a detached Air Force Headquarters function within the Börfink command center and was the primary command post unit for air and missile forces in West Germany.

The primary peacetime mission for the U.S. Air Force F-102 aircraft interceptors controlled by the command center was the identification of unknown aircraft in the Air Defense Identification Zone (ADIZ). This was a thirty-mile-wide zone between Warsaw Pact-controlled areas and NATO airspace. The F-102 Delta Dagger was the world's first supersonic all-weather jet interceptor and the U.S. Air Force's first operational delta-wing aircraft and the first aircraft designed with an all-missile armament, including tactical and nuclear missiles.

In my early briefings, it had been emphasized that the IWO's observations and advices to the Sector Controller in this matter were of extreme importance, not only because of the potential for an international political incident and a threat to military and civilian lives; but, if nothing else, the cost of sending two supersonic aircraft on an intercept in today's dollar equivalent would come to about seventy-five thousand dollars per launch.

On average, two to four interceptor aircraft were activated weekly to respond to perceived immediate threats to identify any intruders into NATO airspace. These were usually commercial airliners or private aircraft that had drifted off course or otherwise violated their flight plans, but there were occasional Warsaw Pact military aircraft intruders and, just before I had arrived, at least one Soviet fighter pilot that had defected to the West and was provided a welcoming escort by two interceptor aircraft. In addition, these interceptor squadrons were tasked to provide assistance to pilots in distress.

Another important mission for the IWO was the observation and control of the three air corridors between West Germany and West Berlin. These limited-access air corridors had been granted as a concession by the Soviets to the NATO forces after the Berlin Airlift had demonstrated to the Soviets that they would not be permitted to isolate West Berlin from West Germany.

Radar controllers at aircraft control posts located at Wasserkuppe and Döbraberg close to the West German side of the border guided both military and civilian aircraft through the air corridor over East German airspace from Tempelhof Central Airport in Berlin and primarily to the Frankfurt am Main civilian airport in West Germany.

As part of the cat and mouse game being played in the Cold War face-off in Germany, U.S. Air Force aircraft would occasionally fly "ferret" missions along the East German border. Aircraft would depart in two waves, about eight minutes apart, flying towards East German airspace at a high altitude and speed. Within a mile of the border they would sharply turn and head back to their home airfield. The purpose of these missions was to cause the Warsaw Pact air defense system to turn on its radars so that the U.S. aircraft could locate and evaluate the Warsaw Pact radar capabilities. Or was it to anger the Russians into a retaliatory intercept attempt, forcing them to violate NATO air space? Any such intrusion by the Warsaw Pact would prompt the U.S. State Department to lodge yet another protest against Soviet acts of aggression. Obviously, another fine example of our tax dollars at work in the implementation of skilled diplomacy.

Likewise, the Warsaw Pact fighters would occasionally head west toward the border at supersonic speed, causing SOC III to scramble fighters in response. Then, when almost at the border, the East German or Soviet fighters would pull up into a vertical climb and roll back toward the east, having tested and evaluated how long it took our fighters to scramble.

At nearby Hahn Air Force Base under SOC III control, there was a special building called the "Zulu Alert" barn near the air base runway. Two fully armed F-102 Delta Daggers were kept ready to take off within a few minutes of a Zulu scramble order. Flight crews and ground-based airmen lived in the two-story Zulu hangar while on Zulu Alert assignment. During a scramble, the flight crew would slide down a fireman's pole from their second-floor living quarters to the aircraft in the hangar. Zulu hangers were also located at the Ramstein and Bitburg U.S. Air Force bases, each with armed interceptors ready to scramble.

We would initiate scramble orders and then the control and reporting staff in the lower level of the Bunker would utilize the so-called "Weapons-Loop," wherein air surveillance data would be transmitted point-to-point from the 412L weapons computer from a ground-based radar site via a data link to the pilots' fire control systems in the scrambling aircraft.

Occasionally, the 412L radar network would detect Warsaw Pact aircraft engaged in the deployment of electronic counter measures (ECM) attempting to test the ability of NATO forces to detect possible targets that might be masked to gain superiority during hostilities. One of the most common types of ECM was radar jamming or "spoofing," often referred to as chaff. This consisted of aircraft or other targets spreading a cloud of small, thin pieces of aluminum, metallic glass fiber or plastic, which was designed to appear as a cluster of targets on radar screens or which would overload the radar with the display of multiple radar returns. On close inspection of the radar system data, we were able to determine radar jamming exercises easily and as a routine activity .

As noted in the description of Watch Officer post duties, the intelligence officers were also responsible for the monitoring of "special interest flights." Special interest was obviously an intentionally vague term used to express something unpleasant or embarrassing or, in the military, it denoted a secret activity. These American spy flights would originate from areas outside the European zones, usually from the continental U.S., and would deploy into the Scandinavian countries north of Germany and then fly parallel to the German border at a safe distance, employing whatever the latest intelligence surveillance equipment or techniques were available.

These were reconnaissance flights from the U.S. Air Force Strategic Air Command (SAC) flying out of Omaha, Nebraska. They had been on missions of global strategic reconnaissance, including photo, electronic and signals intelligence collection. A Soviet intercept and capture of one of these aircraft would have resulted in a major loss of operational advantage over the Soviet forces.

As Watch Officers we were given advance notice of these missions and mandated to observe and protect them from any interception or harm, whether from Warsaw Pact aircraft or from NATO forces who were not provided data to recognize these flights as friendly and might perceive them as suspicious or threatening intrusions.

All of these activities were recorded in the Intelligence Watch Officer log for the day shift, swing shift or midnight shift entrusted to the intelligence officer on duty. Any incident that represented deviations from normal air activity was noted as a FRAGREP, a fragmentary report, to be written in all capital letters in the log. A Fragrep during the Cold War had been defined as, "any occurrence on or near the border which could indicate an imminent attack, provoke an armed clash between U.S./Allied and Warsaw Pact forces or provide the basis for a diplomatic protest from either side."

My Effectiveness Report of November 1968 provided a more detailed description of the Emergency Actions Officer function: "Aside from the duties and responsibilities inherent in the intelligence watch officer position, he is one of a small group of selected individuals responsible for the immediate handling and processing of highly sensitive Emergency Actions messages."

What that actually meant was that, besides all the other responsibilities and actions required of the post, the Intelligence Watch Officer and the on-duty Sector Operations Controller were tasked with the responsibility of being part of the two-man team of nuclear weapons release officers for U.S. forces in Western Europe. On a regular basis, almost every other week and without warning, we would receive notifications to perform simulation drills for the release procedures to ensure that there were no hesitations or errors. While facing the huge map of Central Europe across the room, I found myself simulating procedures that would release the most powerful weapons ever developed on Earth while contemplating what damage that would inflict on the real world depicted on the map before me.

These drills were conducted using a prefix of "white" on the verbalized loudspeaker announcement that would alert all personnel in the Bunker that the procedure was underway. "White," of course, was only a drill, but the importance of a release message from the President of the United States commanded attention from everyone on duty. The procedure consisted of notification from the President being received, authenticated and passed along, which then ordered the release of nuclear weapons as determined by whatever operations plan had been authorized. A "red" prefix meant the real thing. Apparently, and thankfully, no one has ever received and carried out that order.

Since I had been told in one of my post briefings that the Soviets engaged in all the same signals intelligence activities as those conducted by the U.S., I came to realize that this very noisy simulation exercise could easily be picked up as background chatter on open-air communications emanating from the Bunker. This would certainly serve as a reminder and warning of the U.S. readiness to escalate the defense of Europe. This warning to our counterparts on the other side of the border was perhaps the real reason for the frequent Emergency Actions drills that amounted to a very loud rattling of our extremely deadly sabers. The message to the Soviets was loud and clear: We have nukes and we are prepared to use them!

THE CABINET OF CURIOSITIES

AMERICAN AND GERMAN AIRMEN ARRIVING at the Börfink Bunker for the first time were generally amazed when they entered this NATO command center that would be their workplace. It was a massive war room buried under a mountain and filled with many curiosities.

This war room was loaded with technologies that were not well known in the civilian world of the 1960s. In retrospect, it was an oversized Wunderkammer, a German term meaning Cabinet of Wonders, or Cabinet of Curiosities. Developed in Renaissance Europe, Wunderkammers were collections of objects of natural history proudly displayed by rulers, aristocrats, members of the merchant class and early scientists. They were the forerunners to the museums developed in Europe in later years. The Bunker was filled with sometimes classified and often new technologies that intrigued and often amazed its occupants.

The first and most obvious wonder that a newly assigned serviceman like myself would encounter was the forty-foot by forty-foot display screen at the front of the command center. At the height of a four-story building, it was overlaid with a map of Europe focused on the border between East and West Germany. The images displayed on the screen were projected by a machine called a "light valve." This machine took the composite data from the five interconnected radar stations and projected them onto the screen as "moving targets."

The presentation was in color and was also dynamic, showing each aircraft symbol's movement as it was plotted by the 412L computers that had been developed by General Electric. As was to be expected, the good guy symbols were in green and the bad guys were in red (magenta). At that time, this was an astounding development in aircraft control. Decades later, I would recognize that the light valve was the forerunner of projection TV technology.

Another innovation of the 412L system was a new phone system also developed by General Electric that used unique tones to dial the numbers selected on the telephone keypad. Those now-familiar sounds were my early introduction to touchtone dialing. Back home we had been using rotary dial phones where we would select each digit in the phone number being called by placing a finger in a rotatable wheel, one number at a time, at an annoyingly slow pace. It wasn't until the 1980s that the majority of phone customers owned push-button telephones in their homes. In the sixties all of this was available in the Bunker!

The Air Force weathermen on the top tier next to my closed-off top-secret office had a remarkable machine called a thermofax which provided current weather data displayed on a two-foot-wide continuous roll of paper that presented blue contour lines and data looking very much like a contractor's blueprint pouring out in long sheets. The weatherman could often be seen struggling with and untangling great lengths of paper spewing from the machine as he received weather updates. Getting the rolls of paper under control was occasionally accompanied by a few choice words directed at the machine's manufacturer or the paper supplier.

Thermofax was a photocopying technology that was a significant advance in the 1960s since no chemicals were required other than those contained in the copy paper itself. This provided the weathermen with vital data that could be interpreted and relayed to pilots in need of timely forecasts of predicted air pressure and wind speeds in flight zones. At that time, fax machines were unique to major weather services, some news services and a few large corporations in America – yet another wonder.

The technical component of the 412L system used for transmitting data to the U.S. Air Force fighter interceptors was designated as Data Link F-102. It was referred to as "Bandit" data, a term used by controllers to designate unfriendly aircraft. Such data as altitude, heading, speed and number of aircraft were transmitted via voice communications directly to the pilots. Map reference data from the 412L radar sites showing attack angle, speed settings and intercept approaches (cut-off, stern attack, etc.) were communicated via voice to the interceptor pilots, reminding me in later years of the tactical control operations of air assaults against some other empire "a long time ago in a galaxy far, far away...."

Even our snack and coffee breaks presented a modern wonder. There was a small break room in the hallway outside the operations center where soda machines, a coffee vending machine and sandwiches were made available in coin-operated machines stocked by a local German vendor. To heat up the food selection, there was an early countertop microwave oven that could heat cheeseburgers or any other foods that were microwave safe in less than a minute. I usually selected the cheeseburger or the ham and Swiss cheese, not for their taste, but for the convenience and sheer pleasure of operating the machine. These ovens had not yet been introduced in America until later 1967 when their use gradually spread into commercial and residential kitchens everywhere. I had known some busy homemakers who were going to like this convenience!

There had been a humorous occurrence of a French liaison officer who would accidentally blow things up in the microwave at the Bunker on a regular basis. He could not comprehend that putting aluminum foil or uncooked eggs in shells, or other non-microwaveable items in the oven would result in a catastrophe. After each incident, he would be seen pacing around, cursing in French, slightly crazed and talking to himself.

My first use of a computer, on the radar console, was with a trackball mouse, a computer device that was introduced into military radar systems just after World War II. In 1966, an American company, Orbit Instrument Corporation, produced a device called the X-Y Ball Tracker, a trackball that was embedded into the center of the 412L flight control radar consoles. This was a black ceramic sphere about four inches in diameter, a bit larger than a softball. With a movement of the hand over the ball, the operator at a radar console could place a small square cursor over any aircraft being displayed, and then select one of many buttons on the console display board to obtain data. The buttons were labeled with selections for altitude, speed, heading and many other data about the aircraft being queried. This was much easier to get used to and faster than the popular mouse provided on most modern computers.

I was pleasantly surprised when I noted that trackballs had been introduced to personal computers in the 1990s. Large trackballs are still seen on computerized special-purpose workstations, such as military anti-aircraft radars, commercial airliners and submarine sonar devices. These devices had been shown to be more durable and more adaptable for rapid emergency use. Large and well-made trackballs allow easier high-precision work, and are still used in computer-aided design.

From personal experience, I can attest that the trackball mouse was, and continues to be, the easiest and most accurate device for interfacing with a computer. And they're a pleasant reminder of moments when I would glide over to my radar console on my caster-wheeled chair and palm the trackball to acquire the tracking data on an intruding or errant aircraft.

Yet another fascinating device that I encountered was a very limited-edition secure telephone that was located in the intelligence booth. It was about the size of a small refrigerator at three feet tall, with a single touchtone telephone resting on top. I had been told that there were only two of these phones in Europe: the one in my booth that was connected to the other phone located in the highly secured vault about a hundred feet away at the other end of the Bunker command staff tier.

This room, actually a locked vault, was occupied by an Air Force sergeant with a special security clearance who was surrounded by highly classified communications equipment that could never be left unattended. The sergeant (or, as I sometimes wondered, was he NSA staff?) would call me with information when there was important intelligence traffic for me to view within the confines of the secure vault. I would then pass on my analysis of that data to the on-duty Sector Controller.

These calls were made secure by being scrambled in such a way that the originating machine actually broke apart the voice tones that were then reassembled at the recipient machine. They were often very garbled and incomprehensible. When that happened, which was often, I found it was best to walk very quickly and pay a visit to the secure communications vault. At a cost of ten thousand dollars each at the time, they certainly were limited editions and were probably phased out soon after my service due to their ineffectiveness and constant need of repair, my first introduction to the concept of replacing the "mother board" and the propensity of such central connectivity points to require replacement.

The Intelligence Watch booth was equipped with several unique phone systems. The primary phone was connected to the Bunker military communications system that connected further out to other facilities. The system had additional access to the German civilian phone system. The intelligence booth also had an Army field phone with an olive-green-colored metal casing, like one would expect to see at the field headquarters in a combat zone. This phone linked to German border patrol guards who had direct lines to the booth for reporting any unusual flight or other activities near the border. It was sometimes a way to get immediate data from German border observation posts. In an emergency involving aircraft near the border, the patrol guards could call us directly to provide on-site data.

At times on the watch, particularly on the midnight shift, there were prolonged periods of inactivity that would result in a need to fill the downtime. My preferred activity for using this time and staying alert was the study of German history from the Middle Ages through World War II. This provided me some context for the location and the role I was playing in its defense.

Other officers used that time reading fiction, news magazines or whatever else was available to occupy their time. Arriving for one of my day shifts as part our regular rotations in the continuous watch, I was entertained with an amusing tale from one of my IWO cohorts. He had been spending some of the quiet hours on recent midnight shifts attempting to call himself.

He had started out using the land lines that patched him into the line-of-sight microwave relay towers, first connecting to a tower in the Swiss Alps, then south to Italy and the Middle East and across Asia to South Vietnam. Then he connected to Japan and on to Hawaii. He had made it through broken connections and lengthy holds. Getting through the U.S. was the easy part, making the last leg as a quick jump from Washington, D.C., to Air Force headquarters in Germany at Ramstein Air Base, and then directly back into the SOC III Bunker. Joe had called himself, and he was thrilled. He was probably the first and only intelligence officer to circumnavigate the globe by phone.

The booth also had a teletype machine. Teletype technology was not new, but it was unique in that this was the sole connection to a remote U.S. Air Force unit in the basement of Tempelhof Airport in Berlin. This unit of civilian-dressed personnel was named the Electronic Data Processing Facility (EDPF), a deliberately obscure title designed to mask its observation and intelligence functions. Being such masters of duplicity themselves, I'm sure the Soviets were not fooled by this ambiguous title posted on the locked door to a windowless basement office.

Messages from EDPF gave air intelligence updates from up close in East Germany and east of Berlin into Poland and Russia with minimum delay. This gave us a view of air traffic from the heart of East Germany solely reporting directly to the IWO post at SOC III. Data coming in from EDPF always got my immediate attention because they were deeply embedded in and surrounded by the Soviet bloc forces. I always responded to them quickly, because of their strategic location and I was sure that it was lonely down under the airport.

With all of these communications resources available to us, we were well informed of the activities on our front in the Cold War. I can now only imagine what resources and capabilities are available to modern intelligence units, given the developments in computers, satellite imagery and the widespread deployment of telecommunications services developed in the past fifty years.

CURIOUSER AND CURIOUSER

PERHAPS THE GREATEST CURIOSITY I encountered in my Intelligence Watch Officer post indoctrination was something that could not be shown to me, nor had I been given any documentation to study on the subject. This was my introduction to Project Bluebook, an innocuous-sounding title that quickly called to mind the Kelley Blue Book automobile pricing guide. Or was this something more like the Blue Book social registers of polite society in certain American cities? So, what was this Project Bluebook?

I received the briefing on Project Bluebook near the end of my post training, probably because I had not shown any discomfort or voiced any objections when briefed on such subjects as nuclear weapons in Europe that we were responsible for and a brief commentary on local chemical weapons storage in our area of operation. I was now getting briefed on a unique phenomenon that I might encounter occasionally while on the watch. I was told that I could expect to see aircraft that were not friendly and not "bogeys," but simply not able to be identified, and that these aircraft might display unusual maneuvers and flight data, commonly referred to as unidentified flying objects (UFOs).

I was told that Watch Officers were not to allow any U.S. or NATO military aircraft to investigate or otherwise respond to possible extreme anomalies that were viewable and verifiable on the radar system displays. No alarm was to be sounded. No attempt to intercept. We were only to post a log entry, clearly stated and written in all capital letters PROJECT BLUEBOOK with the date, time, aircraft altitude, speed and heading noted, along with geographical coordinates and flight behavior.

At this point in my intelligence career, I had become accustomed to surprising statements and data, but I was now puzzled and somewhat amused by this introduction to what I had long considered to be the stuff of science fiction or the product of overly active imaginations.

In the 1950s, my only introduction to sci-fi and UFOs had been on Saturday afternoons at the twenty-five cent kids' matinees while munching on Milk Duds and Jujubes. Science fiction films such as *It Came From Outer Space* and *The Day the Earth Stood Still* had the young audiences on the edge of their seats. But the most frightening film and still most vividly recollected to this day had been *The War of the Worlds*. When that priest walked toward the alien ship praying, "Yea, though I walk through the valley of the shadow of death," I knew he was a goner.

And now I was an adult getting briefed by a career military officer on how to report the presence and activities of alien aircraft over Western Europe! Why not? I had already been practicing release procedures for the U.S. response to a nuclear attack from the Soviet Union.

When I queried the briefing officer as to why this information was not broadly known and had to be classified as secret, I was told that it was protected information because any acknowledgment of the existence of or factual data about UFOs might undermine the existing social order and possibly lead to unrest in the civilian population.

I could certainly understand this concern, since I was beginning to sense in myself a growing mistrust in those military and government authorities who would withhold this important knowledge. As part of the acceptance of my post duties, I had agreed to uphold the confidentiality of this information and now I was being asked to be a participant in the deception. In the 1960s, that would be easy enough; I couldn't imagine who would have believed me at that time, so it was easy to remain silent on that subject. In the twenty-first century, television audiences have been regularly exposed to popular documentary television programs such as *UFO Files* and *Ancient Aliens*. Of course, there is still no acknowledgment or positive confirmation of UFOs from official government sources.

Over the course of the next two years on my watch, I posted about a dozen Project Bluebook log entries. In each case, the 412L radar system initially detected a single aircraft, heading east to west at enormous speeds, usually in excess of ten to eleven thousand miles per hour. Their altitudes varied from one incident to the next, but they all demonstrated what was recorded as an ability to perform a nearly instant cessation in forward motion. The aircraft would normally hold that position for anywhere from four to ten seconds and then suddenly go into a rapid vertical climb, disappearing when it exceeded the range of our height finder radars.

Since these flights and brief stops were conducted in the general areas of our nuclear weapon-capable aircraft and missile site locations, it had occurred to me that the pilots of these unidentified aircraft might be checking out our capability for deploying nuclear weapons technology. Perhaps they were just making a quick electronic scan or two and a photo reconnaissance run to send updates back to their home base.

The aircraft observed and confirmed by the entire radar network in these incidents had displayed aerospace technological capabilities well in advance of the late 1960s and overshadowed even modern-day technical advances. As a point of reference, in the late 1960s, an American prototype interceptor aircraft had achieved a record-breaking speed greater than two thousand miles per hour. That record was exceeded by about two hundred miles per hour in 1976. Neither of the speeds achieved by these aircraft using modern technologies achieved anything close to the speeds recorded in the Project Bluebook incidents.

As another reference, spacecraft such as the U.S. space shuttles re-entered the Earth's atmosphere traveling much faster than the speed of sound and are said to have been hypersonic. Their usual low-Earth-orbit re-entry speeds have been recorded at nearly seventeen thousand miles per hour while becoming a blazing ball of fire resembling a meteor approaching the Earth at this phase of the landing. In the late 1960s, there were no reports of meteor-like objects visible from or impacting West Germany or anywhere else in Europe during any of these observed incidents.

What I learned through later research was that Project Bluebook had been one of a series of systematic studies of unidentified flying objects conducted by the U.S. Air Force. It began in 1952 and it had two goals:
- To determine if UFOs were a threat to national security, and
- To scientifically analyze UFO-related data.

Thousands of UFO reports had been collected, analyzed and filed at Wright-Patterson Air Force Base in Ohio. However, as a result of an assessment prepared by the University of Colorado entitled "Scientific Study of Unidentified Flying Objects." it was concluded that there was nothing abnormal or exceptional about UFOs.

This study was strictly an academic exercise that was limited to the study of reports by the National Academy of Sciences, previous UFO studies and Air Force experience investigating reports of UFOs. This "Scientific Study" of other studies would hardly qualify as a proper investigation of phenomena according to any scientific method. However, it did deliver a report that would not undermine the existing social order and it did not lead to unrest in the civilian population.

Project Bluebook was therefore ordered shut down in December 1969. Of course, it is highly unlikely that anyone at the University of Colorado had been granted access to classified intelligence logs. And I'm sure that any radar-based reports from the IWO post and similar installations had been dismissed as "unscientific" by the Colorado researchers.

Nevertheless, the results of investigating UFO reports and the conclusions of Project Bluebook by the Air Force were that:

- "• No UFO reported, investigated, and evaluated by the Air Force has ever given any indication of threat to our national security.
- "• There has been no evidence submitted to or discovered by the Air Force that sightings categorized as 'unidentified' represent technological developments or principles beyond the range of present day scientific knowledge.

"• There has been no evidence indicating the sightings categorized as 'unidentified' are extraterrestrial vehicles."

With the termination of Project Bluebook, the Air Force regulations establishing and controlling the program for investigating and analyzing UFOs were rescinded. In other words, "forget what you saw because there's no way to report it." Documentation regarding the former Bluebook investigations was permanently transferred to the Modern Military Branch, National Archives and Records Service, and is available for public review and analysis. I wonder if my dozen or so Project Bluebook log entries ever made it into those archives.

There are a number of universities and professional scientific organizations that have "considered" UFO phenomena during meetings and seminars with the intention of ensuring that evidence is not overlooked by the scientific community, although it is unlikely that these individuals will be granted access to the intelligence logs maintained at command posts throughout the world.

Persons wishing to report UFO sightings have been officially advised to contact local law enforcement agencies. I'd recommend that anyone considering the submission of such a report should be wary of following that advice. Reporting a UFO sighting just might incur a label of "nut job" or "head case" from law enforcement officers or result in an authoritative diagnosis of "delusional disorder" by psychiatrists hoping to acquire new patients in need of adjustment to the existing social order.

MY BIG FAT SECURITY CLEARANCE

INDIVIDUALS BEING ASSIGNED POSITIONS IN the U.S. military are granted security clearances based on the negative impact of revealing, or leaking, the data they work with. The intensity of these background investigations varies, depending on the level of clearance that is deemed necessary for a particular position. Investigations for lower levels of security clearances generally rely on automated checks of an individual's life history, including criminal records, any other negative public or private records, or known connections to criminal, subversive or anti-American groups or individuals.

Investigations for higher clearances become more thorough as the candidates seek access to higher levels of information. As an example, for a secret security clearance, the investigation may require federal agents to interview people who have lived or worked with the individual under investigation at some point during the last seven years.

As part of my briefings for the Watch Officer post, I learned that there are three main types of clearances for security positions in the U.S. military. These are confidential, secret and top-secret. A *confidential* security clearance allows an individual access to information or material that *may cause damage* to national security if disclosed without authorization. A *secret* clearance provides access to information or material that *may cause serious damage* to national security if disclosed without authorization. A *top-secret* clearance provides access to information or material that *may cause exceptionally grave damage* to national security if disclosed without authorization. Each of these clearances, once granted, has to be reinstated for an individual through follow-up background investigations conducted every five to fifteen years, depending on the level of clearance.

I was granted my secret security clearance upon completion of my Air Force officer's training in November of 1966, probably after a brief check for any criminal history. This is routine for U.S. military officers. This gave me access to secret classified files needed for my studies and research at the Air Intelligence School in Denver. By the completion of that training and receipt of my assignment to an intelligence post in Germany, I had been cleared for top-secret security. I only knew that I had been granted these clearances when I was first handed documents for each level of classification. Before I could access any of these documents, I was handed a nondisclosure agreement and told, "Here read this, and, by the way, you're cleared for this now."

In my early IWO post briefings I was also shown documents with security classifications that were the NATO versions for plans, programs and other military activities. These were shared with all NATO military members who had that particular level of clearance. So, there were documents labeled NATO Confidential and NATO Secret, but I never encountered a NATO Top Secret document. Apparently, not everything was to be shared with one's allies.

Since SOC III was part of a NATO command, documents that were excluded from access by non-U.S. NATO members were labeled Confidential NOFORN, Secret NOFORN or Top Secret NOFORN, another way of saying that the material was for U.S. military eyes only. So many types of secrets. But wait, there's more!

Beyond these three primary clearance levels, there was a security clearance that was generally referred to as a "Sensitive Compartmented Information Clearance." In the Air Force it was specifically referred to as an "expanded prefix" that was affixed to the recipient's military occupational specialty code. My Air Force specialty code, as determined by my specialty training in intelligence, had been designated as 8051. Once I had been cleared for access to "sensitive compartmented information," my specialty code would be upgraded to E8051. Such a clearance would provide access to all intelligence information within specified subjects and channels. Such information required special controls for restricted handling of the material and data. In another briefing during my first week on the Intelligence Watch Officer post, I was told that an expanded background investigation was now being conducted on my life as a requirement to perform all the duties of the IWO post in the Sector Operations Center, and that it usually took about six months to complete.

Well, that immediately set me to taking inventory on just how much might be discovered about my conduct as a young man. What about that package of Twinkies I had swiped from the local drugstore after a basketball practice? After all, I was a regular customer and I did pay for the Orange Crush soda, so the druggist did get some of his profit. And then there was that under-age beer drinking at my friend's summer cottage on the island in the bay. After all, who would disclose that? My friends had been just as guilty as I had been. And shouldn't that be offset by my Eagle Scout Award and the school citizenship award I received in my high school senior year?

In later years, I was told by my mother and various friends' mothers that two men had visited them at their homes in my neighborhood. They had been inquiring about my behavior and anything else relating to my character and judgment. Several months after I had started on the IWO post, I received a letter from one of my former college roommates who was now in the Peace Corps. He was curious as to why two men in suits had shown up to interview him about me at his post in Tunisia! That was being very thorough, indeed.

Nevertheless, I was a bit on edge for the next two months until I was finally informed that I had been granted full security clearance for the post; and unusually quickly, I was told. Phew! I could forget about the Twinkie offense. I then received the briefing regarding the expanded clearance and what types of information I would be handling and responsible for. This was the data relevant to the statement mentioned earlier in my performance report that the IWO position "performs other classified duties not describable herein." At this level, I had achieved the access that would be granted to the U.S. President, the Secretary of Defense, the Secretary of State and high-level intelligence officials; but, of course, it would only be for access to the Sensitive Compartmented Information needed for my post functions. Essentially, I would learn a lot but only on a need-to-know basis.

Many years later, in February of 1998, the U.S. Air Force published its "Pamphlet 14-210, Intelligence." This publication stated that, "Signals Intelligence (SIGINT)" was "a category of intelligence comprising, either individually or in combination, all communications intelligence (COMINT), electronics intelligence (ELINT), and foreign instrumentation signals intelligence, however transmitted...." And that, "The NSA is responsible for the US SIGINT program."

That provides a general description of the types of information that I would be receiving, analyzing and acting upon in my intelligence advisory capacity to the SOC III on-duty Sector Controller.

As part of this briefing, I was told that there were very few individuals who qualified for access to this level of information, and that the Soviets most likely already knew that I had been issued this more sensitive security clearance. They would have my name and probably some basic information on my background and education. They would also have noted the call sign of Bravo Romeo that I used to indicate the initial letters of my first and last names used on the IWO post, since I had already been using it in voice communications for the past two months. This call sign was based on the International Radiotelephony Spelling Alphabet, also known as the NATO phonetic alphabet, that assigns code words to each letter of the English alphabet so that combinations of letters and numbers can be clearly pronounced and easily understood. Many of us growing up in the U.S. had become familiar with the use of Alpha, Bravo and Charlie companies for names of U.S. Army troop units in movies and on TV shows set in the two world wars. And now I was Bravo Romeo; it had a nice ring to it.

I addition, I was told that there were known to be about ten thousand spies or paid informants for the Soviet bloc, mostly Germans, operating in the American Zone of Occupied Germany. I was warned to avoid close association with non-U.S.-military individuals and particularly to not engage in any activities such as heavy alcohol consumption or illicit sex that might place me in a security compromise situation. Because the American Zone was actually only about fifty thousand square miles (the size of Alabama), ten thousand East German and Russian agents constituted a significant quantity of locals to be avoided. The simple math: one spy for every five square miles, and probably a heavier concentration in the vicinity of the American military bases.

I was also informed of my travel restrictions that, of course, prohibited visiting Soviet bloc countries and any communist-controlled areas in the world – ever. I was told that if I wished to visit Berlin, I could not use any military or civilian aircraft, but passage on a sealed train could be arranged through East Germany to Berlin. That seemed a bit dangerous and too James Bondish for me. Certainly not worth the effort to visit what was essentially a prison city, so I turned down that offer.

In addition, I was told that there were only certain qualified medical personnel who could attend any procedure on my body that involved general anesthesia. And it was unlikely that any of those medical personnel were stationed in Germany; in other words, it would be better to stay healthy and out of harm's way!

Since I had already been told that it was best to mention nothing about my work at the Bunker, I was now experiencing an even greater tendency toward being overly suspicious and distrustful of others, a condition commonly referred to as paranoia. In fact, a song of the time from Buffalo Springfield reminded me that paranoia does "strike deep" and that "into my life it would creep." And it certainly had. Adding an imposed caution of avoiding close association with foreigners or strangers dictated that I had to restrict any meaningful communications to my fellow workers and other American military service personnel, if even they were to be trusted!

WELCOME TO THE NEIGHBORHOOD

WHEN I FIRST ARRIVED AT the civilian airport in Frankfurt, Germany, I was met by my new boss, Captain Anthony Zilinsky. Tony was an amiable career Air Force officer who had recently served in Vietnam. He was quick to explain that we were driving to my new living quarters in the Hunsrück mountains and pointed out what we were viewing along the way. We rode in his recent model Porsche Super Carrera (SC) that ran smoothly at nearly a hundred miles per hour on the autobahn, an exhilarating ride along a mostly empty highway with no speed limit.

After driving south for about an hour, we left the autobahn and proceeded west into the hills along a winding, mountainous road through a densely forested landscape. Speeding along on tight turns, Tony put the Porsche through its paces and I had now become a Porsche enthusiast, resolving that I would soon acquire one. Finally, we arrived at a more open terrain of low hills and green pastures that would lead us to the U.S. Army's 98th General

Hospital in the village of Neubrücke. I had arrived at my living quarters for this tour of duty.

At that time, Neubrücke (new bridge in English) was a small village with a population of about two hundred residents located along the Nahe (near in English) River in the Birkenfeld (birch field in English) district of the Hunsrück (dog's back in English) mountains in southwestern Germany. See, you're learning German already!

This was farm country at an elevation of about thirteen hundred feet above sea level. It had long been home to one of the poorest populations in Germany, including the period when it was used for extensive military facilities and fortifications by the German army and air force in World War II. As part of the original division of the Occupied Zones of Germany after World War II, the Birkenfeld district had been located in the French zone, later to be taken over by the Americans for administration and defense in 1949.

The buildings for the 98th General Army Hospital were constructed on a one-hundred-and-ten-acre parcel of land on a small hill just above the Neubrücke train station in 1954. Soon after construction began on the fifty-five-building complex, the Army Corps of Engineers discovered that the site had been the location of twelve large earthen mounds, a Celtic burial ground. The remains and relics were immediately transported to a museum at the nearby city of Trier, Germany's oldest city, before the hospital was completed.

Once fully constructed and equipped, the hospital had at its disposal a variety of specialty clinics in a thousand-bed facility, about twice the size of most urban hospitals in the U.S. in modern times. When first established, four hundred enlisted men and two hundred officers, doctors and nurses provided medical services. The hospital had been set up to provide a rear lines evacuation facility as a part of contingency planning in the event of World War III. In anticipation of that, a complete hospital train was kept standing by at all times. Fully equipped to provide emergency medical services and evacuation of the wounded from any front lines battle location, doctors and nurses participated in weekly transport exercises to ensure combat readiness. Fortunately, the train and the massive hospital facility were never needed.

When I arrived in 1967, there were only a few doctors, nurses and enlisted men caring for about a hundred patients, most of whom were part of the wounded soldiers evacuated out of the Vietnam conflict or servicemen and their families from neighboring military facilities requiring medical services.

A short walking distance down the road from the Army Hospital at Neubrücke was the U.S. Army's Boehmer Airfield in the town of Hoppstädten. This former Luftwaffe airstrip had housed Messerschmitt 109 fighter aircraft during the war and now serviced several American H-13 observation helicopters, but mostly handling the large Sikorsky H-34s for troop transport and search and rescue actions.

When the U.S. Army took over the airfield in 1961, they found German Luftwaffe anti-aircraft gun emplacements off the western end of the runway, positioned to protect the airfield from Allied air attacks. The main military housing barracks, dining hall and motor pool had also been left over from the German air force.

Along with other locations in the Hunsrück area, this airfield had been a forward Luftwaffe aircraft fighter base that had flown under the cover provided by the surrounding hills that were frequently concealed by fog, rain and snow. Luftwaffe bases in the area were sometimes intentionally obscured using camouflage, even some with runways painted to blend in with surrounding terrain. These became known to American reconnaissance pilots during World War II as "hidden airfields."

In the 1960s, hikers into the hills and pastures surrounding the Hoppstädten/Neubrücke valley would discover blown-up concrete bunkers from anti-aircraft weapons positions on the Siegfried Line that protected the airstrip. The hikers would also discover wreckage from German aircraft that had failed to negotiate safe returns from missions against Allied forces. A "hidden" air base can work either way in dense fog: difficult to locate and difficult to land on safely.

This was part of the Siegfried Line, referred to by the Germans as the West Wall during World War II. It was a defensive line built between 1938 and 1940 that stretched for almost four hundred miles and featured more than eighteen thousand bunkers, tunnels and tank traps. The network of defensive structures stretched from northwestern Germany on the border with the Netherlands and continued south along the western border of the old German Empire to towns along the Rhine River down to the border with Switzerland.

Near the close of World War II, from September 1944 to March 1945, the West Wall was subjected to a large-scale Allied offensive, with an initial onslaught of more than a hundred thousand mostly American soldiers thrown against these fortifications. The overall cost of the Allied victory in this campaign alone was close to one hundred and forty thousand American lives.

The first military bases in the Baumholder area had been established around 1000 B.C. by Roman invaders. Since then, the area had gone under German administration and military control and occasionally under periods of French authority. During my time of service in the area, the most prominent U.S. military facility in the Birkenfeld district was the U.S. Army Garrison (USAG) Baumholder located about nine miles from our living quarters in Neubrücke.

Baumholder became a modern military facility around 1937, when the massive build-up of German military forces required the construction of dozens of bases throughout the country for training activities. The initial Baumholder facility encompassed nearly thirty thousand acres, an impressive size for that time and the largest training facility in the German army. The location was chosen for its varied terrain that included valleys, hills, forests and open fields. Over eight hundred local families had to be relocated and thirteen villages and fourteen farms were obliterated in the development of this vast training site.

Baumholder became a garrison town when the Wehrmacht (literally the "defense force") built its barracks and troop training grounds on the site. The Wehrmacht was the title of the unified armed forces of Nazi Germany from 1935 to 1946. Among many Wehrmacht units, the Baumholder training area was used by the German Afrika Korps Panzer Division led by General Erwin Rommel. Between 1941 and 1945, the troop drilling ground was also the location of a prisoner-of-war camp for Soviet and Polish military and other prisoners.

Immediately following the end of World War II, the first American unit to arrive at the Baumholder facility was an armored division consisting of tanks and armored personnel carriers, essentially replacing the facility's former armored occupants. During that same year, a massive reconstruction was started that provided multiple facilities for both the troops and their families. The USAG Baumholder now hosted the largest number of U.S. forces outside of the continental United States. This amounted to about four thousand soldiers along with their wives and children, totaling more than thirteen thousand Americans in the Baumholder community.

At times, when I was driving on the country roads in the area, it was easy to imagine that we were still operating in an active war zone. Tanks would suddenly lurch up unexpectedly onto the roadway, providing a test of a driver's reaction time. Convoys of armored personnel carriers and trucks loaded with equipment and hardware could stall traffic longer than one might expect from a herd of sheep or pigs, which also had to be expected on these roads!

Although my posting was in the Bunker at Börfink, for administrative purposes I had been attached to the U.S. Air Force air station located in Birkenfeld, about four miles east of Neubrücke and about nine miles west of the Bunker. The station had no aircraft or weaponry but served as a dining, berthing and administrative facility for enlisted personnel working at the Bunker. The arrival of the 615th Aircraft Control & Warning Squadron in 1962 had commenced a decade-long buildup of Birkenfeld Air Station and its related facilities that supported those Air Force personnel posted at the Börfink Bunker.

The station had some small administrative offices, a U.S. post office, a small store (called a base exchange in the Air Force) a very small officer's club (actually a bar), an airman's club and berthing for single enlisted men. Across the street from the air station was a picnic area and an American baseball field.

The buildings and infrastructure of Birkenfeld Air Station had first been established by the German army as an anti-aircraft artillery battery with the arrival of an artillery unit from Berlin in 1938. The unit consisted of approximately two hundred men and fifty vehicles. Its proximity to the nearby Luftwaffe airfield in Hoppstädten provided anti-aircraft artillery along the line of defense from anticipated Allied forces air attacks.

This was the background and heritage of the area surrounding my new home: military airfields, a massive armored vehicle training site, ammunition dumps, command posts and missile sites. Essentially, the West Wall had been rebuilt, maintained by the United States and NATO forces; instead of facing enemies from the West, it was now facing an enemy to the East: the Soviet Union's Warsaw Pact.

MY HUMBLE ABODE

AFTER A BRIEF STAY IN transient berthing in the officer housing area on a hill overlooking the Army hospital, I was transferred to the nearby Bachelor Officers Quarters (BOQ), a major upgrade from my transient room that had provided only enough space for a dresser and a single bed. My new residence was one of the four, three-story apartment buildings on the property: one for male officers, another for female officers and two more for medical doctors and their wives.

The BOQ for men housed the officer's club restaurant and bar on the first floor, an ideal location for the primary consumers of large quantities of food and alcohol: the young male officers on the floors above. Most married Air Force and Army officers lived in nearby subsidized housing rented from the local German residents resulting in only about ten male officers in residence at the BOQ.

Across the street from the BOQ for men was a comparable building for women. This included about ten Army nurses and two female hospital volunteers. The volunteers were referred to affectionately and respectfully as "candy stripers," a term derived from the red-and-white-striped pinafores they wore that resembled thinly striped candy canes. Pinafores were sleeveless dresses, tied or buttoned in the back and typically worn as a jumper by female volunteers in hospitals in the U.S. at the time. The candy-stripers performed support functions such as reading to patients, passing out magazines and providing comfort and conversation to patients.

The nurses were all female registered nurses and officers in the Army Nurse Corps. When on duty, they wore classic starched white uniforms, white nylon stockings, white shoes and white Army Nurse Corps caps.

There were two senior officers, veteran nurses in charge of the nursing unit at the hospital. These were older women who had somehow avoided marriage while operating in an environment with an overabundance of eligible males. It was no wonder actually. These two senior officers came across as generally unfriendly in demeanor and aloof from the other officers' club patrons who were in their early twenties.

All the other female patrons of the club were friendly, healthy-looking and active American girls who had created lives of adventure for themselves by volunteering to apply the skills of their chosen careers. They were now posted in a foreign country in a predominantly male world with little or no orientation to the German culture, customs and language. They were from all over America and many thousands of miles away from their families and friends and now living in a BOQ for women. Not exactly girls "born to be wild," but definitely "looking for adventure in whatever came their way."

On days off, many of the young male and female officers became tourists for the day, visiting medieval castles that might be encountered in the larger villages, wineries along the Mosel River and local village stores and markets, even trips to the annual Grand Prix at the Nürburgring racetrack, and to other popular tourist attractions in such cities as Old Heidelberg and Munich.

The officers' club dining room served breakfast, lunch and dinner seven days a week to accommodate the Bunker officers and the hospital nurses who were residents of the BOQs and who were all on rotating shifts to provide twenty-four-hour coverage for their posts.

The dining room had several small tables for up to four diners, with one longer table that accommodated up to eight diners at once. Dining was the primary social event at the club during the day and the bar was open at night. Most of the young officers and nurses would dine together at the large table, providing many opportunities to chat about their new lives in Germany, sharing knowledge about the area and stories about their experiences off the military bases using the local community resources, referred to as "on the economy" in military jargon.

Less than a week after my arrival, a nurse new to the hospital joined a group of us for lunch at the long table several spaces away from where I sat. Blonde, blue-eyed with a broad smile and a pretty face, I listened quietly as she told an enthusiastic story of her first shopping trip on the economy.

She then asked if anyone at the table knew German, or could read German, as she displayed a plant she had purchased in a local store. This was a bromeliad plant provided with growing instructions written in German. Bromeliads are tropical plants in the same family as the pineapple, and certainly not native to the mountains of southwest Germany.

I had never seen or heard of a bromeliad, but this was my chance to impress a pretty girl with my German skills, so I volunteered a translation. I made my way through the instructions without too many stumbles and pauses and succeeded in gaining approval from this attractive and optimistic nurse named Chris who had taken on the improbable task of cultivating a tropical plant on a mountain range well-known for its cloudy and rainy weather, accompanied by sleet and snow in the winter months.

A few days later, I met with two new friends I had made at the officer's club bar, Andy and Jeanine. They were a young American couple who lived on the economy, and I found that they were always fun to talk with. He was an Army captain who commanded missile units at the Bunker and his American girlfriend, Jeanine, was a civilian nurse at the Army hospital.

While we sat in the comfortable chairs of the club bar, I was being amused by some of Andy's stories about the Birkenfeld area. He switched the subject when he told me that Jeanine had mentioned that she had been working with a nurse I should meet and that we would get along well. In just a few minutes, I was introduced to that same Chris by Andy and Jeanine. We all had some drinks and arranged a double date for dinner at an Italian restaurant in the village of Kusel, about seventeen miles down the winding mountain road.

At the restaurant, Andy recommended that Chris try an item on the German menu called schnecken, which I knew to be escargot, a delicacy encountered in my college days. Chris was not familiar with schnecken (escargot in French and snails in English) and Andy, an Austrian-American fluent in German, translated it to snails and dared her to try them. Chris, up for the challenge, didn't hesitate and found she actually enjoyed this exotic dish very much. I was starting to enjoy this young woman very much, and I began to envision more road trips in our future.

By that time, I had moved into a third-floor apartment in the BOQ. The rooms were somewhat spacious for military quarters as they had been designed ten years earlier probably for two or more officers sharing each of the two rooms on either side of the large bathroom. That meant that I had a bedroom with an oversized single bed on the left, a bathroom in the middle and a living space with a comfortable chair and sofa on the right.

Chris and I had started spending much of our off-duty time together. With her radiant smile that made my heart leap and a sense of humor shown in her enjoyment of my sometimes lame attempts to amuse, she had won me over. Add to that her very attractive legs revealed by her mini-skirt, and I realized that I was smitten, which at least sounds like a German word for being hit with something, which I had been.

Since my apartment was obviously too spacious for one person, and this was the liberated 1960s, along with our discovery of our mutual hormonal surges, we decided to move in together. Chris brought over her civilian clothes, including her mini-skirts, her uniforms, other personal effects and an impressive record collection from her apartment across the road. Since we were both officers, we were not guilty of fraternizing with enlisted personnel, so no infraction of the Uniform Code of Military Justice there.

Our mutual interest in the latest music grew while we were out on road trips in the countryside and on the German highways, autobahns without speed limits! Chris and I kept up-to-date with the wave of British and American popular music along with some of the "underground" music of the era. This music was not carried on local German radio and certainly not on the Armed Forces Radio Network.

Randomly searching on the car radio dial, we were able to pick up the latest music from Dutch-language Radio Veronica, an offshore vessel located in international waters off the coast of the Netherlands. It had begun broadcasting in 1960, and continued for more than fourteen years while becoming the most popular radio station in the Netherlands. Such radio stations operated outside any territorial limits to avoid government restrictions and were appropriately called "pirate radio." After a few months of listening to the high-speed chatter from Dutch disc jockeys, I began to understand some of what they were saying, at least enough to work out their over-the-top enthusiasm for the latest tunes from Britain and America.

That prompted more road trips to some of the larger villages in the area where we could locate the most recent albums being imported into Germany, usually from Britain. We found the best resource for new records was a store just fourteen miles away from Neubrücke in the picturesque city of Idar-Oberstein, considered to be the capital of the German gemstone industry. The store carried the latest album releases from Britain in slick varnished sleeves that distinguished them from the imports out of the U.S.

Also at that time, the greatest and most memorable acquisition for our record collection came from Chris' record club selection mailed to us from the U.S. When we received and first heard The Beatles' *Sgt. Pepper's Lonely Hearts Club Band*, we were amazed by its unique and complex tunes, poetic imagery, social commentary and uninhibited good fun. We listened to this album repeatedly in our third-floor BOQ room, discovering greater depth and meaning on each play. When first released, the *Washington Post* had declared,

"Music may never be the same again." It had certainly begun to change what Chris and I and so many others expected from music and the way we looked at the world around us.

* * *

The third floor of the men's BOQ was quiet and very private with only one other resident on that level. At the other end of the hallway lived Colonel Gustav Rödel of the German Air Force. He had been pointed out to me while I was on duty at the Bunker and I had seen him occasionally on the command dais. I had observed that each morning he was picked up at the BOQ in a German air force sedan driven by a uniformed German Luftwaffe airman. As neighbors, we saw each other only occasionally in the third-floor hallway but he never spoke to me and only once nodded in my direction.

My initial encounter with Colonel Rödel had been by way of an invitation to an informal get-together of Bunker officers at the Birkenfeld Air Station officers' club. As a new officer in the unit I felt it appropriate to attend this event and socialize with the other officers. I was comfortable with the conversations about German beer, wine and weather and enjoyed speaking with many of the senior officers with whom I had worked on a regular basis at the Bunker. Then, the guest of honor stood up and announced that he would be showing some aerial film footage. I was surprised to learn that the event's featured entertainment was provided by my neighbor, Colonel Rödel.

He commenced showing live-action, black-and-white footage of his fighter aircraft attacking several U.S. Army Air Force bomber aircraft with machine-gun fire and downing at least one of them. The display was greeted with murmured approvals from the group of officers in the small bar.

During the course of this display, one of the senior officers, an American bomber pilot veteran of World War II, called out, "Hey, that's me, that's my plane." A ripple of light, nervous laughter swept across the room. Not being comfortable with this camaraderie among former enemies, I felt the urge to get out of the confined space of the bar and excused myself for a promised date with Chris.

I later learned from conversations with senior officers at the Bunker that Colonel Rödel at the age of twenty-five had been a recipient of the Knight's Cross with Oak Leaves, one of the highest awards in the military forces of Nazi Germany during World War II. The Oak Leaves clasp attached to the Cross was awarded for leadership, distinguished service or personal gallantry.

Rödel's record was impressive. He was credited with ninety-eight victories (referred to as "kills" in the U.S. Air Force) in his nine hundred and eighty missions. He recorded one victory over the Eastern front. The rest of his ninety-seven victories were recorded over the Western front against British and American aircraft and twelve of those were four-engine bombers.

Later in 1943, his unit had moved to Germany for the defense of southern Germany and Austria against the U.S. Army Air Force's 15th Air Force bombing raids. This was most likely the source of the film footage that he had shown us at the officers' club. In 1944, he led his command into the Battle of Normandy and claimed his ninety-eighth and final victory, far exceeding the ten confirmed aerial victories qualification to achieve fighter Ace status.

Gustav Rödel became well-known and admired for an authoritative command to his men in World War II when he stated, "You are fighter pilots first, last, always. If I ever hear of any of you shooting at someone in a parachute,

I'll shoot you myself." His refurbished Messerschmitt 109 fighter aircraft has now been placed on display at the Military History Museum at the Gatow Airport in Berlin.

In 1957, Colonel Rödel reentered military service in the West German Air Force. After completing training courses in the U.S., he was assigned to the Air Defense Division at NATO's Supreme Headquarters in Paris. While not mentioned in available published records, Colonel Rödel spent more than a year in a liaison function on the command level dais at the Börfink Bunker. I never saw him engage in conversation with any other officer on the dais, but I was usually only paying attention to the Warsaw Pact air traffic. As an observer, he was most likely being prepared for his final service position as Commander of the Second Allied Tactical Air Force in northern Germany and he retired from military service with a final rank of brigadier general in 1971.

Eighteen years earlier, in the summer of 1949 at the age of five, my neighborhood friend Woody and I had dug out a foxhole in his back yard to play American Army soldiers at war with the fearsome Nazis. Using sticks as our rifles and rocks for grenades, we took turns wearing his dad's U.S. Army helmet and held off the Nazi onslaught, defeating the enemy in just three days of pitched battle, with breaks for meals and sleep. We emerged victorious, exhilarated and without injury, but our maternal superior officers were infuriated by the mud on our clothes and the dirt in our shoes, ears and hair.

Now as an adult, my neighbor down the hall turned out to have been a highly decorated Nazi war hero. I had grown up in a world with values and codes that seemed to lack direction and consistency. I was definitely through the looking glass and down the rabbit hole in this military game and it was all still sounding to be uncommon nonsense to me.

WE'RE NOT IN THE U.S. ANYMORE

THE U.S. MILITARY FACILITIES AT Neubrücke, Birkenfeld, the Börfink Bunker and the Baumholder Army Garrison were all located in the Hunsrück mountain range of southwestern Germany. The name of the range originated in ancient times and was originally referred to as "Hundesrucha," the back of the dog.

Growing up in southern New England in a state bordering on the Atlantic Ocean was a far cry from my new home in the mountain forests and farm lands now occupied by an odd mixture of farmers with oxen and pigs and American military defensive forces. My home state carried the appropriate nickname of "The Ocean State" where every resident was less than a thirty-mile drive to the four-hundred-mile shoreline. America's Cup yacht races, tuna fishing derbies, lobsters, swordfish steaks, clam chowder, coffee ice cream and hundreds of sandy beaches provided a local flavor that was not to be found in the Hunsrück mountains. But my new home did provide a wide variety of locally made sausages including bratwursts and knackwursts seasoned with sharp mustard on small rolls that could be ordered from food trucks along the side of the forest roads away from the villages. They served simple fare that featured French fries served with mayonnaise, *pommes frites mit mayonnaise* (the French influence), and no ketchup, all of which made for some great on-the-go lunches. Andy and I once confounded the bartender at the Hoppstädten gasthaus when we ordered wienerschnitzels, breaded veal cutlets in the Viennese style, and slices of bread, and then proceeded to make our own American-style sandwiches – a delicious alternative to the hamburger!

This was the southernmost mountain range in western Germany, bounded by the Rhine River in the east, the Mosel River to the north, the Saar River in the west, and the Nahe River to the south. In fact, a part of the Nahe passed along the edge of the Neubrücke Army Hospital property where I lived.

The undulating Hunsrück plateau extended about fifty-five miles in a southwest-to-northeast direction. The range was twenty to twenty-five miles wide and had an average elevation of thirteen hundred to sixteen hundred feet above sea level. It extended across several higher ridges including its highest peak, the Erbeskopf, reaching nearly twenty-seven hundred feet in elevation, an excellent location for an early warning radar station for military defense.

The climate was characterized by rainy weather, often with a rising mist in the mornings, something to be careful of along the winding road on the Bunker commute. I proceeded with caution in those dense morning mists and had a few close calls with the local red deer when driving to and from the Bunker, but I paid close attention and could stop on a dime when needed.

The area was generally cloudy and wet with the cloudiest part of the year from October to the end of March. The wetter season lasted eight months, from mid-May to mid-January, with a greater than thirty percent chance of rain or snow on any given day.

The snowy period of the year lasted for four months. With my knowledge of basic German, I came to see an irony in the use of the German word Wetter (meaning weather and pronounced vetter) as a dominant descriptive characteristic of this area. Excuse the pun, but the Wetter here was very much wetter than I had ever experienced or ever wanted to experience again.

My initial encounters with local Germans in the area exposed me to a dialect of German I had never encountered in my German language studies in school. Hunsrückisch was a West Central German dialect that did not undergo all the change phases to High German because it had been influenced by neighboring languages through the centuries.

For example, the locals said wat (English what, German was), mudder (English mother, German Mutter) and zwo (English two, German zwei). I very soon encountered difficulties with the local dialect when I first attempted to make a simple purchase of gasoline using coupons for American military personnel that I had purchased at the Birkenfeld Air Station. The young German attendant at the gas station inquired if I had "zwo Benzingutschein." I knew "Benzin" (gas) and "Gutschein" (coupon), but what was this "zwo"? After a reversion to sign language, I was able to pay the young man. I had just learned that I would not be refining my spoken German language skills on this tour of duty.

The lower plateau regions of the Hunsrück had been cleared of much of their natural forests centuries ago and had been used primarily for raising cattle and other livestock, while the highlands were covered with extensive beech and spruce forests.

Small villages have long been the predominant form of settlement in the Hunsrück with farmhouses forming an integral part of the village along with the local church or the gasthaus (literally the guest house, or inn).

Unlike the farmhouses we were familiar with in the U.S. with a main house and barn centered on a large property measuring hundreds of acres, farmhouses in the Hunsrück were usually lined up in a row on both sides of the village road, built wall to wall. Looking closely when slowing down as I drove through the small villages in the area, I would notice that farmhouses were the predominant structures.

Village farmhouses were constructed so that both the family and the livestock could live together under one roof, the family on one side of the building and the livestock on the other. During winter months, the bodies of the livestock served as a natural heat source and also provided a vital component for the farmhouse' compost heap. A seemingly practical arrangement, but I thought I'd have trouble sharing my home with the threat of a potential methane leak from next door.

Access to the street was only possible through the front of the house. I would frequently observe the women of the farmhouses scrubbing the front door steps early in the morning. I wondered at and admired their extreme dedication to cleanliness.

The free space between the road and the front of each farmhouse was used for stacks of firewood, equipment for fieldwork, and the often towering manure piles. I saw heaps of manure by the roadside that sometimes exceeded twelve feet, and later learned that the size and height of the pile was to be recognized as a public demonstration of the industriousness of the farmer. This was strange to encounter when driving through the villages, unless one knew that the farmer's land was often not at the back of his own house. He had to transport his tools and his natural fertilizer from his compost pile to fields that were sometimes as distant as five miles away, so the edge of the road made for an efficient storage yard.

The village streets often had no run-off channels to direct the heavy rainfalls, at times turning front yards into mud puddles formed from the runoff of the manure piles. When the farmer drove his cattle out into the pastures each morning, cow dung sometimes covered the road with the pungent odor pervading the vehicle of the unwary traveler. If the manure piles did not dry out completely during a wet summer, I learned that it was sometimes best to roll up the car windows until I had exited the village. The dedicated scrubbing of front steps could now be seen as a sensible measure of domestic hygiene.

Many of the country roads that connected the villages were originally constructed in the Middle Ages or earlier and did not use the technique of banking the outside road edge on tight turns, making it difficult to stay on the road, particularly in wet and snowy weather. Modern engineers bank the curves of roads towards the inside of the turn so that cars do not have to rely solely on friction between the car's tires and the road surface in order to round the curve. The original roads in this area were designed to accommodate horse carts, carriages and oxen-drawn farm vehicles and did not take into consideration vehicles entering turns at thirty to seventy miles per hour.

An additional driving hazard I encountered frequently on these roads was a condition known as black ice, or

Glatteis (smooth ice in German) as printed on many road signs in the Hunsrück. These were patches of nearly invisible slippery road surfaces. As soon as I had acquired my first vehicle a few weeks after my arrival, Tony gave me a briefing on local road hazards. Yes, I had acquired my own Porsche SC from a U.S. Air Force pilot being transferred out of the country from the nearby Bitburg air base! Tony advised me to drive with caution, particularly over the low areas in the road where the fog could freeze over. During his driving safety indoctrination, Tony informed me that I had replaced a young officer who had driven his newly acquired sports car off one of the unbanked curves, landing within the top half of a tree with disastrous results.

After driving in the Hunsrück for a while, I noticed that I didn't have to worry about crashing into any utility poles, because there were none! This was a pleasant absence from the landscape for someone who had been brought up in suburban America. The effect of the undergrounding of all utilities was most noticeable for me in later years when I returned home and actually noticed for the first time the visually cluttered skylines of American towns and communities.

Telegraph cable undergrounding began in northern Germany as early as 1870. I had been told that the undergrounding of all utilities in Germany had been the result of the predisposition of Germans to prepare for military conflicts and the need to secure communications and electrical power lines in the event of future hostilities with their European neighbors. The completion of the Rhineland cable undergrounding project in 1921 had been hailed as a clear demonstration of the superiority of German science and technology. It also enhanced the establishment of their westernmost defenses for future conflicts.

Aside from the aesthetic and military benefits, it had been shown that undergrounded utility lines were less susceptible to outages during high wind thunderstorms or heavy snows or ice storms, or even damage from the occasional drunk driver making high-speed, unscheduled stops at utility poles along the road.

The Hunsrück area had been opened up by the construction of a dense network of roads during the nearly four-hundred-year occupation of the area by the Romans. In the final years of the decline and fall of the Empire, the neighboring Franks conquered the Roman territories and divided them up. This was the start of the great western and central European empire of Francia and also the beginning of centuries of territorial conflicts throughout Europe.

In the mid-eighth century, the area was divided into smaller districts; then, in the Middle Ages, the Hunsrück was further fragmented between various counts and archbishops, along with a number of other lesser rulers, continuing a long history of conquest and domination by neighbors. Not a good place to visit and certainly a difficult place to survive easily.

During seventeenth-century central Europe, the Hunsrück suffered through the Thirty Years War, a religious and political war that was one the longest and most destructive conflicts in European history, with eight million casualties. At the end of that war in 1648, Louis XIV of France then made reunification demands on the Hunsrück and other principalities in the area. Their failure to comply resulted in yet another war with the French king's troops invading and thereby precipitating the Nine Years War with the main fighting taking place around France's borders with the German Rhineland, specifically in the Hunsrück area. Continuing this chaotic struggle of war and destruction, this led to the War of the Spanish Succession, from 1702–1715.

Finally, in the years immediately following that series of wars, the area experienced a respite from conflict. Trade and commerce in the Hunsrück had been given an opportunity to grow, with mining and ore smelting industries prospering. As an extension of this success, there was an increase in local manufacture of implements for the home, farming and handicrafts: ovens, pans, boilers, weights, spades, nails, hammers, anvils, looms, spinning wheels and, of course, cannonballs and shells. A stable economy had begun to emerge, but only temporarily. War would soon return.

After an absence of war for nearly eighty-years, the seizure of power in France by Napoleon with his expansionist policies resulted in French troops once again invading the territories west of the Rhine, and in 1792 the Hunsrück was annexed to France. Which brought to mind the appropriate lament from Ray Charles that "if it wasn't for bad luck, there would be no luck at all." The people of the Hunsrück knew this too well.

After the withdrawal of the French occupying forces, a severe economic situation impacted the Hunsrück during the years 1815-1845. A poor harvest in 1815 was followed by what has been referred to as the "year without a summer" in 1816; grain prices rose rapidly and 1817 became a year of famine. The farm communities essential to survival in the Hunsrück suffered greatly during this period.

Fortunately, in 1822, having just achieved independence from Portugal, the Brazilian government sent a German doctor back to his native Germany to recruit mercenaries and colonists who were needed to stabilize this new South American country, the fifth largest in the world. Many of them were recruited from the Hunsrück and surrounding areas. The first immigrants settled there in 1824 in what is now the Brazilian state of Rio Grande do Sul and they have remained a vibrant force in that country for nearly two centuries, even retaining their unique Brazilian Hunsrück Portuguese-German dialect known as Hinsrick.

Two decades later, with all of Europe beset with inflation, crop failures and social unrest, especially in 1846 and 1861, many residents in the Hunsrück decided to leave in two more waves of emigration, specifically to Brazil and North America where they were able to break away from the cycles of war and poverty in their home land and finally enjoy prosperity in new worlds with greater freedom and opportunities.

Then, in the first half of the twentieth century, those who had remained in the Hunsrück and their offspring would experience the impact of yet another phase of suffering and oppression from military conflict and control in the area when it served as the defensive stronghold and offensive staging area for the two world wars of the twentieth century.

SKELETONS IN THE CLOSETS

AFTER WORLD WAR I AND the Nazi rise to power, the massive German military build-up became a major presence and activity in the Hunsrück mountain range. The military construction projects could not have escaped the attention and participation of the local residents. In my limited encounters with Germans in the area, I had sensed a reticence, a holding back and fear that I had not expected to experience with the locals. This was not the merry and jovial Germany that I had imagined in my youth, having listened to recordings of *The Student Prince* operetta with the Heidelberg University students joyfully raising their ornamental beer steins in rousing toasts to drink and romance.

This was a region that had been stuck in the aftermath of oppression while witnessing destruction and carnage and was now surrounded at every turn by the military forces of its conquerors.

The sense of fear and sadness that I perceived among the locals reminded me of the suffering and hopelessness described in the first adventure novel in the German language, *Simplicius Simplicissimus*, inspired by the events and horrors of the Thirty Years' War in the seventeenth century in Germany. The subtitle of the novel told the story: "The account of the life of an odd vagrant ... namely where and in what manner he came into this world, what he saw, learned, experienced, and endured therein; also why he again left it of his own free will." His solution had been to cut himself off from mankind by choosing the life of a hermit. This novel had been assigned reading in my advanced studies in German literature at Yale with a professor who had been a drama critic in Berlin before the Nazis came to power. We had mostly studied twentieth-century German plays, but I believe we had learned more about life in Germany in our study of *Simplicius Simplicissimus* than from all the stage plays of Bertolt Brecht and other popular twentieth-century German playwrights.

My Army friend Andy was a great source of information about the local area. He would occasionally explore the area surrounding Hoppstädten and had once stumbled upon a Jewish graveyard less than three miles east of the village on the slope of the Eborner mountain. He came across nearly two hundred Jewish gravestones marked with dates from as early as 1770. On the older part of the graveyard, there were sandstone tomb slabs with fragments of Hebrew inscriptions preserved on their faces.

Andy, with his German fluency and his friendly but slyly inquisitive manner, asked some of the local residents and gasthaus patrons whether there had ever been Jews residing in Hoppstädten, suspecting that this would have been kept a secret in this village. He did receive uniformly negative responses, until one bar patron confided that before the outbreak of the war on one late night, military vehicles rolled into the village and transported all of the Jews from the area, never to return to Hoppstädten. I was beginning to understand some of the sadness and restraint that I had encountered in this community reminding me of what Simplicius had experienced and endured in this world.

Learning this, I researched other major developments in the Hunsrück during World War II that had not been mentioned in local literature or in the briefing sheets supplied to American servicemen newly assigned to the area. I discovered that by 1937 German military forces had become interested in the Hunsrück region as a strategic deployment route to the German-French border along the Siegfried Line, building a series of fortifications on the western border of Germany, Hitler's "impregnable" West Wall mentioned earlier in this story. By September 1938 more than half a million men were working on the West Wall, and approximately a third of Germany's total annual production of cement went into constructing three thousand concrete pillboxes (concrete guard posts with loopholes to fire weapons), bunkers, and observation posts.

A new Hunsrück Highway, eighty-seven miles long, had been built in just a hundred days and provided a strategic route leading from Koblenz in the north of Germany over the Hunsrück mountain range to the West Wall.

The roadway and the other fortifications on the Wall were constructed in 1938 by a branch of the German Labor Front that had been established as a construction camp in the vicinity of the village of Hinzert, about twenty miles away from Neubrücke and the Luxembourg border. While driving through the mountains it is likely that I had passed Hinzert without noticing it since not a lot of attention gets directed to such infamous locations.

The Labor Front was the Nazi trade union organization that had replaced the independent trade unions in Germany after

Hitler's rise to power. The Third Reich had not only nationalized all trade unions, but made membership mandatory, forcing every worker to join the state-operated union. Initially, Hinzert had served as a "work camp" for laborers on the West Wall.

During 1939 the camp was taken over by the Todt Organization, a civil and military engineering group in the Third Reich, named after its founder, Fritz Todt, an engineer and senior Nazi figure. The organization was responsible for a huge range of engineering projects both in pre-World War II Germany, in Germany itself and in the occupied territories from France to the western Soviet Union during the war. The organization became notorious for using forced labor. During the late phase of the Third Reich, the Todt Organization administered the construction of all concentration camps that had been set up to provide forced labor for German industry. Perhaps it was an appropriate coincidence that "Tod" in German translates to "death" and is pronounced as "Todt."

Under Todt Organization management, Hinzert was used as a "training camp" for individuals detained by the police. Hinzert was no longer a "work camp" for West Wall workers; it had now become the center of the completed "West Camp," a police detention facility that reported directly to the Inspector of the Security Police and the Security Service, an intelligence agency comparable to the Gestapo, the official secret police of Nazi Germany.

From its beginning in 1941, nearly fourteen thousand prisoners were transited to the Hinzert concentration camp. The first prisoners were German workers who had demonstrated "anti-social behavior" providing "labor education" to those who were "work shy," and others who had been deemed socially undesirable. They were put to work on the construction of the West Wall in the Hunsrück.

The camp was later used to host forced laborers from occupied countries, mainly Luxembourg resistance fighters and French dissidents. Other prisoners, forced laborers and POWs, were sent from Poland and the Soviet Union. Many Hinzert prisoners were used as slave laborers in the surrounding region, including units stationed at satellite camps on the outskirts of Neubrücke and Hoppstädten, the two villages that I had been able to view from a third-floor window of my quarters. These "workers" performed maintenance tasks at air bases such as the airfield at Hoppstädten, and also worked on marsh drainage and forestry projects.

Prisoners at the Hinzert concentration camp were subjected to harsh conditions. The camp was operated by the SS (short for Schutzstaffel or "protective shield"), an elite corps of combat troops. A branch of the SS, the Death's Head Unit, ran the concentration camps and extermination camps. A great many prisoners were tortured and murdered at Hinzert, often shot, drowned or killed by lethal injection. Some SS guards tortured prisoners or left them to die of sickness or hunger. They were then buried in the nearby forest.

The exact number of victims murdered at Hinzert remains unknown. In 2005, a memorial and documentation center was established on the site of the former Hinzert concentration camp, where those prisoners who were not sent home were buried and memorialized.

* * *

At the close of World War II, in a demonstration of the mutual cruelties so often perpetrated by the participants in any war, the U.S. Army established camps to hold captured German soldiers in the Hunsrück town of Bretzenheim, about forty-four miles from Birkenfeld. Later called the

"Field of Misery," this was one of the Rhine Meadow camps, a group of nineteen camps built in the Allied-occupied sector of Germany after the war.

Officially named Prisoner of War Temporary Enclosures by the U.S. Army, the camps held between one and two million surrendered Wehrmacht personnel from April until September 1945. As might be imagined, this would have presented an enormous logistical problem, but as early as 1943 it was decided that German prisoners held in camps would be designated as Disarmed Enemy Forces, not Prisoners of War (POWs).

That decision had been made by the Supreme Allied Commander in Europe at the time, General Dwight D. Eisenhower, so that the Allies would not have to be governed by the Geneva Conventions regarding treatment of prisoners. By not classifying the hundreds of thousand of captured troops as POWs, the problems and costs associated with proper treatment and care of so many prisoners were greatly diminished. Yes, that is the same Eisenhower whose wartime leadership had evoked the successful "I Like Ike" campaign and who twice won election as President of the U.S. from 1953 to 1961.

The spacious camp at Bretzenheim covered an area of five hundred acres divided into twenty-four separate "cages." In 1945, it contained more than one hundred thousand prisoners while under the command of the U.S. Army. For another three years under French occupational authority, it was reduced to only eighty acres as a camp for war prisoners. Hundreds of thousands of prisoners funneled through this camp, with some being released to their homelands and others transported to France for forced labor.

An outrageous number of prisoners did not survive the camp, dying of hunger or falling victim to illnesses. This was greatly contributed to by the absence of shelters that should have been constructed inside the prison compounds, as they would have been if the Geneva Conventions had been followed. These agreements between countries form the core of international humanitarian law, regulating the conduct of armed conflict and protecting people who are not engaged in hostilities and those who are no longer doing so.

Under the circumstances of neglect experienced by the "Disarmed Enemy Forces," the deaths of soldiers in the camps totaled many thousands who died from starvation, dehydration and exposure to the elements. The exact number of deaths has never been determined.

A monument at the site commemorates the camp and its occupants, revealing yet another example of the tragic consequences of war in the Hunsrück, adding Allied neglect of military prisoners at Bretzenheim to the Nazi atrocities at the neighboring Hinzert concentration camp.

ALARMING INCIDENTS

A MAJOR CHALLENGE FOR THE U.S. and Allied forces after World War II was how to look as deeply as possible into the Soviet Union and the other Warsaw Pact countries without getting caught. Of particular interest were the quantity, capabilities and existing locations of air defenses, radars, anti-aircraft weapons, surface-to-air missiles, and locations of bombers and aircraft fighter planes.

To accomplish this, starting in 1946, the U.S. Air Force launched reconnaissance missions that collected signals intelligence (SIGINT) including communications (COMINT) and electronic (ELINT) intelligence, and photographic intelligence (PHOTINT). Reports of overflight reconnaissance had been classified under the heading of Special Compartmented Intelligence (SCI), but in 2012 they were declassified and released by the National Security Agency, the U.S. agency responsible for the collection of SIGINT, encompassing the other "INT" varieties listed above.

Overflight and peripheral reconnaissance missions were conducted with great secrecy. During my service, these missions over Europe were generally engaged in peripheral reconnaissance, from a distance that would not place an aircraft in harm's way. The SIGINT missions especially were very secretive because of the character and importance of the information and the methods that were employed in obtaining data.

The U.S. provided cover stories for these missions, reporting some as weather reconnaissance, navigational training or access along border areas for mapping. In other cases, the U.S. would acknowledge a mission to be a photographic mission but the other equipment they may have had on board was not divulged. The Strategic Air Command (SAC) put SIGINT equipment aboard its PHOTINT missions as a means to protect the flight and also had SIGINT personnel positions aboard all their reconnaissance aircraft to protect them; that is, to get an idea whether and how the Soviets were reacting to the mission. SAC aircraft would also intercept ELINT signals as a means to fine-tune their electronic counter-measures tactics and equipment designs.

It was standard procedure for the Soviet air defense forces to scramble fighter intercept aircraft when American reconnaissance flights approached their borders. They were very quick to label a non-Soviet aircraft as "unidentified," then upgrade the threat to "hostile" once identified as a U.S. aircraft, and then as an "intruder" if it penetrated Soviet airspace. During my years on the Watch I had observed that the Soviets were not very discriminatory in their labeling of aircraft that constituted a threat to the Warsaw Pact. On several occasions, I had observed Soviet interceptors chasing after aircraft that had drifted across the border at speeds of about one hundred and twenty miles per hour. These were most likely private pilots who had lost their bearings, or even crop dusters who had been picked up erroneously on Soviet radar. We would closely monitor these errant aircraft that were about to be intercepted. They would then get warned and directed back on course by the German air traffic controllers, and most likely reprimanded when they returned to their airfields.

Between 1950 and 1964, the Soviets made thirty documented attacks resulting in shootdowns of U.S. reconnaissance aircraft. There were additional attacks on other NATO member aircraft on similar missions, but specifics have not been released on those encounters. Even allies don't like to share their mistakes.

The most notable of these shootdowns was that of U-2 pilot Francis Gary Powers, who was shot down and captured in 1960 while on a high-altitude reconnaissance flight deep inside the Soviet Union. The U-2 was a special high-altitude aircraft that flew at a ceiling of seventy thousand feet, thought to be out of altitude range for the Soviet interceptor jets at the time. The capture of Powers, known as the U-2 Affair, resulted in the cancellation by the Soviets of a conference with the U.S., Great Britain, and France regarding administration of the two Germanys. The Cold War was definitely growing more solidified and more dangerous after this incident. With all the intelligence sources available to the U.S. Air Force, sufficient warning and guidance now had to be provided to reconnaissance missions, and they were.

As part of the Intelligence Watch Officer job description mentioned earlier, we were to "monitor special interest flights," meaning that we would be given exclusive advanced notice of any reconnaissance aircraft coming into our area and we would watch out for them as a first priority. Any reconnaissance is a mission to obtain information by visual observation or other methods about the activities and resources of an enemy. Aircraft are particularly useful in this endeavor. The areas of interest for air reconnaissance of "special interest" actually extended along the German border up into the Scandinavian countries and down to Switzerland, as well as any reconnaissance aircraft sent into the three flight corridors to Berlin within East Germany.

Whenever a reconnaissance flight was scheduled for peripheral reconnaissance along a portion of the German border, we would be given advance notice by the Strategic Air Command that a flight was scheduled to operate in a specific area. I had been briefed that these strategic reconnaissance flights originated out of SAC headquarters in Omaha, Nebraska, about seven thousand miles away from our location in Western Europe, a great distance requiring mid-air refueling during the mission.

More frequently, we would be given advance notice of Pan American Airways "civilian" aircraft entering one of the Berlin corridors. On the command dais, both of these reconnaissance flight activities were referred to as "one of ours" by the intelligence officers and "one of yours" by the Sector Controllers. The informal-sounding description for these flights arose out of the need to speak openly on the dais without putting attention on the secrecy of these missions.

The corridor flights were able to provide intelligence updates from a height of ten thousand feet while moving across the twenty-mile-wide air corridors. By the time I had gotten on the Watch post, the pilots had been engaged in this reconnaissance for many years, so they were highly skilled at drifting off their flight plans within the corridor restrictions without attracting attention. What sometimes looked like sloppy pilot performance was most likely an attempt to create an expanded area of coverage for photo and electronic surveillance within East Germany. The pilots gave us some moments of anxiety, but because of their expertise and alertness, we never had any alarming incidents with those flights.

As an Intelligence Watch Officer I was tasked with advising the Sector Controller of any flights that went off course or if Warsaw Pact fighters were in a flight's vicinity, or any other intelligence that indicated possible danger. Occasionally, with the information resources available to the Watch post, we were able to warn of possible hostile intent by the Soviets so that a mission could be aborted or take evasive action if required. With these cautionary actions in operation after 1964 in Europe and throughout the U.S. sphere of influence, there were no more shootdowns.

However, there is always the possibility of human error in any activity that depends on precise execution under the stress of secrecy and possible hostile interference. There can be human error arising simply from a lack of good sense or judgment, as well.

It happened one evening that I was on duty paired with a Sector Controller who had still not obtained the expanded security clearance required for him to be apprised of these SAC reconnaissance flights. We were on a swing shift and I had been informed that a special flight would be arriving in the airspace north of Germany that night. It was a SAC flight from the U.S. and I noted its arrival into our radar coverage exactly on schedule.

The 412L system was not able to determine the identity of the flight, thereby activating the system's bright white warning light, providing the alarm that an intruder had entered into restricted airspace. I informed the Sector Controller that the flight was authorized and it was "one of ours." The newly posted and uninformed Sector Controller was not going to pay attention to advice or take an order from a young lieutenant. After all, he was the senior officer and a decorated pilot who had survived World War II.

He disregarded my advice and ordered a scramble of two interceptor aircraft against the "intruder." Without raising my voice to the senior officer seated in the Controller's chair, I put my face close to his and quietly and firmly warned that there would be serious consequences if that flight were intercepted and identified. During the moments of his hesitation, I imagined the worst case scenario: that the Soviets might also run an intercept resulting in both U.S. and Soviet fighter aircraft seeking out a Strategic Air Command reconnaissance aircraft as an intruder. The Sector Controller looked from me to the screen and back to me again.

He picked up his microphone and cancelled the intercept order, perhaps surprising himself in doing so. Of course, as a standard procedure, this incident had to be reported in my log. The senior officer was removed from his post the next day. His lack of good sense would no longer present any danger to the defense of West Germany.

* * *

The Nike Hercules was the surface-to-air missile (SAM) used by U.S. and NATO armed forces for medium- and high-altitude long-range air defense. It could also be used in a secondary surface-to-surface role, and had the ability to hit other short-range missiles in flight.

These missiles were normally armed with W31 nuclear warheads, rated at the lower end of the range of nuclear weapons at about two kilotons. To compare the force of the W31, the Little Boy atomic bomb dropped on Hiroshima was rated at sixteen kilotons. Several W31s from a single Nike Hercules battalion could amount to a comparable force to the drop on Hiroshima and might wipe out whole cities, large military facilities or a squadron of twelve to twenty-four attacking aircraft. Nike Hercules was developed to carry a nuclear warhead in order to defeat entire formations of high-altitude supersonic targets, such as might be anticipated in missile or aircraft attacks from the Soviets.

As mentioned earlier, all Hawk and Nike Hercules battalions and their associated mission control centers were interconnected for tactical control in the integrated communications network that provided accurate data from the entire NATO early warning system These were monitored by the Army missile control personnel directly below the command level dais in the Bunker,.

Since the Army missile commanders were on the next level below the command staff on the dais where the Watch booth and the Sector Controller were located, we would occasionally hear the young Army officers as they drilled procedures for various responses in battle scenarios.

On a quiet afternoon after a year on post, anticipating an end of the shift followed by some live communication and a good dinner at the officers' club dining room, I heard, very faintly, the voice of a young Army missile commander below me authoritatively call out a command with the word "red" in it. On hearing that, I became very alert and hoped I was mistaken. "White" is always a practice run for any procedure; "red" is the real thing, indicating an actual attack sequence for a missile launch.

In the next half minute, I received a call on my booth phone from the sergeant in the secure intelligence vault who had some urgent intelligence for me. He calmly stated to me that the Soviets had detected the action of our Army missiles being elevated and directed toward the East German border. In an apparent response, the Soviets had ordered a counterattack readiness, raising their missiles toward us.

I quickly proceeded from the vault back to the Sector Controller and, not wanting anyone to hear that I had such information, particularly the French and German observers, I whispered to him that the Soviet missiles had been placed in actual battle positions.

I also told him about my hearing the use of "red" in the Army missile exercise. He immediately called down to the Army lieutenant and cancelled the order. The Soviet's excited "chatter" quieted down and all missiles on both sides were lowered and returned to their resting positions. Without another word, the Sector Controller and I both let out simultaneous breaths of relief and I returned to the Watch booth.

The young Army officer was apparently dismissed from his post, as I never saw him at the Bunker again. Obviously and correctly, there had been no tolerance for errors in a command position in the Cold War.

This was another case of Army FUBAR that my Army friend Andy had warned me about. The term stood for Fouled Up Beyond All Recognition, with the F word usually exchanged with another word in the common U.S. Army usage, not an expression that I had encountered in my military training. In the Air Force's understated reporting style that I had become familiar with, this event might have been referred to as an "incident with an unexpected and undesirable outcome."

Andy's use and explanation of the term FUBAR had accompanied an amusing and somewhat scary tale of Army incompetence in which he told me about an incident of the actions of two Army missile officers at a remote missile battalion location who had been placed in a panic by an upcoming inspection and inventory review from headquarters staff.

To be on the safe side, they conducted their own inventory and discovered that they had an extra missile in the inventory! Even though it was not equipped with a warhead, how would they get rid of an actual missile? Launch it off into the ocean or to a vast wasteland? No, it would be detectable by radar. And it was too large for a trash bin. So, they came up with the only solution: bury it! Under the cover of night, they manned two shovels, dug through until morning in a wooded area and laid it to rest, perhaps still buried and undisturbed.

* * *

Systems malfunctions and human errors were always potential threats to the delicate balance that had been achieved whenever U.S. and Soviet forces faced each other during the Cold War. The close call between U.S. Navy warships and a Soviet submarine during the Cuban missile crisis in 1962 was one such incident that nearly tipped our countries into World War III.

Another such incident would occur in the European theater of operations in 1983. Russian Lieutenant Colonel Stanislav Petrov was the duty officer at the command center for a Soviet nuclear early-warning center that was reporting that five missiles had been launched from the U.S. and were headed toward Russia.

Petrov determined that the reports were a false alarm. Rather than reporting to his superiors that the enemy was launching a nuclear strike, Petrov correctly estimated that the "attack" was really a glitch in the system and instead informed his superior officers in Moscow that his equipment had been malfunctioning – he hoped!

Petrov has now been credited with having prevented an erroneous retaliatory nuclear attack on the U.S. and its NATO allies that most likely would have resulted in full-scale nuclear war. Subsequent investigation confirmed that the Soviet satellite warning system had been mistaken. No missiles had been approaching and the computer detection system was creating a false alarm by a rare alignment of sunlight on high-altitude clouds above North Dakota in the U.S.

Years later, Petrov said that at the time he was never sure that the alarm was erroneous and that his civilian training helped him make the right decision. He said that his colleagues were all professional soldiers with only military training and, following instructions, would have reported a missile strike in progress if they had been on his shift. Indeed, the Soviet top leadership, with only a few minutes to decide and being informed that a U.S. missile attack had been launched, would have made a decision to retaliate with a nuclear counterattack.

After the incident, Petrov underwent intense questioning by his superiors about his judgment in not passing along this alarming report. Initially, he was praised for his decision but soon after was reprimanded for improper filing of paperwork when he had not described the incident in the war diary. He received no reward and was reassigned to a less sensitive post and took early retirement from the military.

In later years, when details of the incident emerged in Western media, he was showered with praise and hailed as "the man who saved the world." In 2004, he was awarded a thousand-dollar prize for his contributions to mankind from an American group. Two years later, he was invited to appear before the United Nations, and in 2012, he received the German Media Award and in 2013 Petrov was granted the thirty-two thousand dollar Dresden Prize for averting World War III. Thank you for your outstanding contribution to mankind, Stanislav Petrov!

* * *

False alarms are too regularly generated when tensions run high in direct military confrontations such as during the Cold War. Occasionally, we observed East German or Soviet fighters heading west toward the border at supersonic speed, in an attack formation, causing the SOC to scramble fighters.

When these "bogeys" (hostile aircraft) approached in close proximity to the border and sometimes overflew the border, the East German or Soviet fighters would usually pull up into a vertical climb and then roll back toward the east. This was a routine test of our readiness, providing the Soviets data on our response time from the moment of detection to the actual scramble of our interceptors. Ironically, it also told us how efficiently our Zulu Alert interceptor aircraft were responding for procedural training and possible corrective actions.

But in the spring of 1968, during an uneventful midnight shift, suddenly, at around 2:00 a.m., I was called to the secure vault and given a typed message that indicated that a simultaneous take-off of about twenty aircraft out of western Russia had occurred and had not yet shown up on the Bunker's display screen and radar scopes.

Back in my booth, I received an urgent telex message from our Electronic Data Processing Facility unit from below Tempelhof Airport in Berlin. They had acquired radar signals of about forty aircraft from Russia and Poland, and warned that they were about to confirm that more were coming. By then, the first wave of these flights began showing up on the Bunker's giant display screen.

Before the first few aircraft had reached within a hundred miles of the border between West and East Germany, I had counted more than forty aircraft, spread apart, but all flying in the same westerly direction.

Moving at a steady speed of about four hundred miles per hour, these were most likely Tupolev Tu-95 strategic bombers that were intended to deliver free-falling nuclear weapons and, in a test years earlier, had dropped the Tsar Bomba over a testing range in the northern Arctic Circle – the most powerful thermonuclear device ever detonated.

The bombers were soon joined along their route by more aircraft taking off just east of Berlin. These were most likely MiG-21 supersonic fighter aircraft that would provide escort functions in defense of the bombers.

This was either an exercise at a magnitude that exceeded anything described in my training briefings or it was the first wave of an actual attack against the NATO forces in Western Europe.

A silence had descended in the Bunker operations room as all personnel stared at the growing mass of magenta aircraft markers heading past Berlin toward West Germany, filling the eastern half of the display screen.

Was this the start of World War III?

The display screen showed that the aircraft were not in formations that could easily access NATO primary targets but were headed directly toward our greatest defensive concentration of anti-aircraft missiles and rapid response interceptor aircraft. Continuing that approach would have resulted in their immediate destruction once we confirmed any actual hostile intent.

I had seen their air operations tactics enough to know that this was a "spoof," a deception to get NATO forces to respond, an attempt to reveal our tactics and capabilities, some of which were still classified as top-secret. It had all the markings of the same old cat and mouse game, only on a larger, more frightening scale than we had seen before.

I went immediately to the Sector Controller on duty. He looked at me expectantly, preparing for a description of a worst-case scenario. I assured him that the swarm of aircraft crossing over East Germany was not a threat; at least I was mostly sure, still watching intently at the actions of the swarm of aircraft. As I finished the explanation of my statement, the first of several leading aircraft started to turn away from the border, peeling off from the formation.

The Sector Controller, still sitting forward in his chair, transfixed in his view on the display screen, asked again if I was sure. I was more certain now, and repeated my assurance. He agreed, and then sat back in his chair in relief as the "bogeys" peeled away to the north or south, then headed back east.

A few of the Soviet aircraft had missed their turns and actually penetrated West German airspace, but none of our Zulu Alert interceptors had been scrambled and no missiles were raised and set to their launch positions.

This was the longest report I would ever write, as this was certainly a massive "occurrence on or near the border which could indicate an imminent attack." I had done my duty in defense of Western Europe at no cost in human life through a counter-attack against enemy aircraft and without escalation to a higher level of hostility. Since all such reports had to be printed in non-cursive letters by hand, my shift ended with some stiff fingers but with the satisfaction of having performed well in an intense situation.

For the Soviets, the entire operation was a bust – a total waste of fuel and wear and tear on a fleet of aircraft that had drawn absolutely no response from NATO forces. They must have wondered how we knew that it was all a sham – or perhaps they thought we had been sleeping! They'll know now, if they read this.

* * *

In the first week of August 1968, representatives from the Warsaw Pact countries met on the other side of the

Iron Curtain in Bratislava, Czechoslovakia, and signed a declaration that affirmed "unshakable fidelity to Marxism-Leninism and proletarian internationalism" and declared an "unrelenting struggle" against "bourgeois ideology" and all "anti-socialist forces." That kind of heavy-handed declaration was a certain indication that there were cracks in the system somewhere and some patch-up work was now desperately needed.

The results of these talks were determined to be unsatisfactory by the Soviets, bringing into play its policy of demanding the governments of its satellite states to subordinate their national interests to those of the "Eastern Bloc." The Soviets would enforce this policy through military force as needed.

During the night before and the early morning of August 21, 1968, Eastern Bloc armies from the five Warsaw Pact countries, the Soviet Union, the German Democratic Republic, Bulgaria, Poland and Hungary, invaded Czechoslovakia. That night, two hundred thousand troops and two thousand tanks entered the country.

The first troops occupied the International Airport near Prague, where their deployment was unimpaired. The Czechoslovak military forces were immediately confined to their barracks and surrounded by the Soviet troops until there was no threat of a counter-attack. By the morning of August 21, Czechoslovakia had been occupied.

I was very surprised when I showed up for my shift that morning. The communication lines were very active on the dais and in the IWO booth, but mostly from other units requesting confirmation of this stunning display of Soviet military force.

The day after the invasion, I was asked to review any data we had received that might have warned us of an imminent invasion that had occurred just a few miles east of the West German border that we had been sworn to defend. The other Watch officers covered my shifts while I spent a week inside the vault scanning through the special intelligence data.

I had already been familiarized with the interior space of the vault when I first received my expanded security clearance. The room was filled with electronics equipment in steel casings that resembled filing cabinets standing about four feet tall. These units received and processed data provided from the various sources of signals intelligence routed to us.

My initial indoctrination to the contents of the vault consisted of learning my responsibilities to protect and, if needed, to destroy the equipment to ensure its security. There were two sledge hammers and a large axe readily accessible for the physical destruction of the units. In addition, each cabinet had a destruct cord near its top that, when pulled, would release a phosphorous incendiary device that would burn through the layers of the equipment, thus denying access to the information and technology by any intruder. The vault also contained .38-caliber handguns that were available for denial of unauthorized access to the vault and the equipment. The Watch Officers and the enlisted staff in the vault had been sworn to protect this equipment with their lives.

As I got into the task of researching the SIGINT traffic during the time leading up to the invasion, I began to realize that the entire system was suffering from information overload, handling a continuous barrage of information from sources all over the world. Actually, most of the intercepts received were centered around the battle action in Vietnam, a sort of play-by-play to satisfy the interests of fans of the U.S. home team. There were also fragments of data from Europe and, of course, the usual major league baseball scores hot off the wire services from the U.S. According to a report about SIGINT in the 1960s, the NSA had determined many years later that, "the volume of unprocessed ... tape was becoming difficult to manage technically and was embarrassing politically."

After a one-week search through thousands of pages of intelligence traffic, I was able to locate sufficient evidence that a Warsaw Pact military invasion had been in the final stages of preparation at least a week before the actual date of the incident.

In its later review of the invasion, the NSA reported, "SIGINT helped U.S. intelligence monitor developments in the Warsaw Pact. During the summer of 1968, SIGINT reporting coming out of NSA clearly showed that growing numbers of Soviet and Warsaw Pact troops were being deployed along the borders of Czechoslovakia."

Reports may have been sent and received, but obviously no one was paying close attention. Once again, an overabundance of data had most likely smothered the actual significant intelligence that would have revealed the intended Soviet invasion.

The NSA report went on to state, "The invasion did not take the White House by surprise (it had 'strategic warning'), but the CIA did not provide advance warning because CIA analysts refused to accept the possibility that the Soviets would invade the country (although a minority believed otherwise)."

So, the NSA had determined that the CIA was guilty of misadvising the President, now that the NSA was able to prove from my research that all the relevant data had been reported through its military acquisition of intelligence. Politics, as usual, in Washington.

In my Officer Performance Report following this incident, the Detachment Commander, Lt. Colonel Thomas Forsythe, submitted an additional endorsement on my behalf: "He has proved to be a very effective and competent Intelligence Watch Officer who has made a valuable contribution to the mission of this unit. He has made careful analyses of significant intelligence events and presented them in such a manner that rapid evaluation could be made of the information."

There was no question that the Colonel was referring to the analyses reported from my research into the invasion of Czechoslovakia. Obviously, that report had been well received by the NSA in that it had provided an interpretation of its data reporting as evidence that the intelligence had been made available. Of course, it had been rendered useless because it had not been noted or acted upon in a timely manner.

A FRIEND IN THE NEWS

WE WOULD OCCASIONALLY RECEIVE MAGAZINES that were passed around the Bunker, usually helpful in fighting off the slow periods during a swing or mid shift. Such magazines as *Sports Illustrated*, *Time* and *Life* might show up months after their publication dates. In January of 1968, I came across a delayed edition of *Time*. Leafing through it showed nothing of interest until I noticed a short article with a photo and caption. The young man in the photo looked familiar and the caption stated that this was Dee Owen, a friend from my high school days. We had played football and basketball together, and enjoyed each other's company during our sports activities. Dee was a friendly, intelligent and energetic team member and he had always given his all in any activity. I had thought of him during my college years, recalling the pleasure of his company, and now he was the subject of a national magazine article.

The *Time* article was titled: "Youth: Unanswered Questions." With a dateline of Friday, Sept. 15, 1967, it read, "Life was never dull for Dwight Hall Owen Jr. By the time he was a sophomore at Stanford University, gangling (6 ft. 4½ in.), energetic 'Dee' Owen had fought forest fires in the West, mined gold in Honduras, motor-scootered through Europe, and worked his way to Viet Nam. There, as a freelance newspaper correspondent, he became something of a hero by shooting it out with the Viet Cong when the 1st Infantry patrol he was accompanying was ambushed north of Saigon (*Time*, Dec. 17, 1965)."

An earlier 1965 *Time* article had reported that, "At breakfast time on a jungle road in Vietnam last week, Dwight Owen killed a Communist and saw dozens of Americans die." That was the first time most people had heard of the Stanford sophomore who had given up his academic pursuits to see the war in Southeast Asia. "Owen had been walking down a path with a 1st Infantry Division unit when several machine guns opened up," the article continued. "Two soldiers died instantly in the attack. Owen quickly took cover, where from his vantage point he saw movement in the darkness of the jungle. 'Then it moved again,' he told *Time*. 'I fired six shots. No more movement.'"

"In lucid detail, readers learned that Owen spent the night after the 1st Infantry battle, 'in a moonlit foxhole half filled with water, surrounded by the death-black jungle.' During the night, Owen thought about the wrist watches still ticking on the dead soldiers' wrists, about the GIs whose heads had been blown off, and, surrealistically, about the booze fests at Stanford fraternities. 'I thought about mother and dad and a girl back home,' he told the *Time* reporter. 'And I thought about my country and my own people.'"

As I read his account of the attack and Dee's response to defend himself under attack, I wondered if I would have taken a similar action, taking the life of another. Dwight

Owen, who had made friends easily, who sincerely cared about others and who so often provided an uplifting presence in any human interaction, was an unlikely candidate to participate in combat or take the life of another. This would not have been part of any scenario he would have envisioned for himself as a non-combatant in a senseless war. He likely would have seen this as an act worthy of remorse, as I would have.

On September 13, 1967, an article in the *National Catholic Reporter*, an unidentified girl who first met Dee Owen in 1965 at Stanford was interviewed in the *Reporter* article: "His life did offer an alternative to the way a person can criticize the war," she said.

"There were a lot of things in the system that Dee didn't like, but he wanted to be in a position to influence the U.S. policy in Vietnam. Dee did a lot of things that people who are willing to burn their draft cards would not. He had to go where the action was – he joined AID [the Agency for International Development] to work within the structure, but he didn't feel limited by the structure. ... Dee had a grasp on life that I think a lot of people never have. ... He was filled with a vitality, that after talking to him, you couldn't help but bring some of it away with you.

"When he was there [in Vietnam] the first time he became very caught up in the war and the Vietnamese people and what the war was doing to their country.... He went back the second time with a job to do; it wasn't just a sense of adventure, but a feeling of commitment."

A press release from AID, reported that, "Funeral services [were conducted] for Dwight Hall Owen Jr., 21, was killed while doing humanitarian work in Vietnam.... on August 30, 1967 by Viet Cong small arms fire close to a village near a coastal city in Vietnam. He was working for AID, which was sponsoring economic development in Vietnam as well as giving medical and humanitarian aid to the victims of the fighting. Owen was an assistant to the AID Provincial Representative and was principally concerned with community development.

"Owen graduated from the Moses Brown School in Providence in 1964 and had completed two years of Asian and Political Science studies at Stanford College in California. He had worked for AID from February to August 1966 and returned there for another year's work last month. He had intended to return to Stanford in the fall of 1968."

Dee Owen was the product of an unusual educational experience developed and provided by the Society of Friends for more than two hundred years at Moses Brown School in Providence, Rhode Island. In the 17th century, George Fox, the founder of the Religious Society of Friends, encouraged its early members to "live adventurously; let your life speak."

At Moses Brown, Dwight Owen and I, along with thousands of other young men over more than two centuries had been given the opportunity to gain knowledge and develop competence in an environment that fostered trust, integrity and kindness toward one's fellows. The type of education championed by the Friends was directed at embracing and bettering the world. This was imparted to us not in the preaching of specific religious beliefs, but by way of example in dealing with others and through encouragement in the search for truth in all our studies and endeavors.

It came as no surprise to me that Quakers had played a leading role in the women's suffrage movement and pacifist movements in the United States. Later in life, I was pleased to learn that the Society of Friends had received the Nobel

Peace Prize in 1947. The Prize had been awarded to the Society of Friends for its relief work with the victims of war and famine after World War II. They had provided assistance where needed in Germany, elsewhere in Europe and in Asia, as they had in previous wars.

In the award presentation speech, the chairman of the Nobel Peace Prize Committee spoke with appreciation of their work in public campaigns for peace over the centuries: "The Quakers have shown us that it is possible to translate into action what lies deep in the hearts of many: compassion for others and the desire to help them – that rich expression of the sympathy between all men, regardless of nationality or race, which, transformed into deeds, must form the basis for lasting peace. …they have shown us the strength to be derived from faith in the victory of the spirit over force."

Dee Owen, while not a member of the Society of Friends, had certainly "lived adventurously" and had shown that same compassion for others and a desire to help. I was saddened by Dee's passing, as well as by the loss of other friends to the Vietnam War. They had deserved to continue their adventures, bringing hope and joy into the lives of all those they would have encountered along the way.

UNLOCK AND LOAD

I WAS INTRODUCED TO NUCLEAR warfare at the age of ten when my fellow students and I viewed a film shown in public schools that displayed the blast of white light and the towering mushroom cloud that was followed by a ferocious blast of air and debris sweeping into the desert landscape, blowing away telephone poles, wooden sheds and badly constructed houses.

Between 1949 and 1955, the Soviet Union had detonated eighteen nuclear weapons over its testing site in the Arctic, including its first hydrogen bomb in 1953. As a result of this intensified Communist threat, school children throughout the United States were instructed and participated in mandatory Cold War Nuclear Bomb Drills. The program included black and white film footage from earlier U.S. nuclear tests displaying the destructive power that might sweep across our communities and into our classrooms just as they had in the Nevada desert as shown in the films.

In 1954, my fellow fifth-graders and I were very impressed but mostly frightened for our futures after viewing the film. At an age when our lives should have been filled with great promise now that the Nazi menace had been defeated, we were now forced to contemplate an almost otherworldly overpowering force similar to what we had seen in the final scenes of the sci-fi disaster film *When Worlds Collide*.

Having viewed the magnitude of the threat on the nuclear bomb test film, we were then given the simple solution provided by the Civil Defense official visiting our school. Dressed in a fireman's dress uniform this official showed us how to perform "duck and cover" drills that might save our lives in the event of a nuclear attack. We were told to get under our desks to avoid falling ceiling panels and light fixtures as soon as we heard the civil defense siren that warned of approaching danger. Just crawl under your desk, tuck in your head, arms and legs, and turn your head away from the windows to avoid the flying shattered glass.

He assured us that the wooden desktops would protect us. We then had to demonstrate how we would duck and cover to save ourselves. We followed his orders and experienced the discomfort of getting down on our knees under our desks, down below the wads of bubblegum and crudely scratched initials.

I had been paying close attention to the film and had realized that these drill procedures appeared to be an unlikely defense against what looked like certain death to all in the path of the blast.

Thirteen years later in my classroom at the Air Intelligence School in Denver, Colorado, the instructor showed my class of about twenty Air Force officers and three Marine officers the same nuclear detonation test film. But this version was without edits, a kind of director's cut for adults. It included the devastation of even more phone poles, sheds and more badly constructed houses, but it also depicted Army Jeeps, armored personnel carriers, tanks and fully dressed mannequins being tossed along the desert floor like tumbleweeds in a desert storm.

This version of the film also included footage of the devastated landscape of the city of Hiroshima and included still photos of initial blast victims and the subsequent effects of those directly in contact with the bomb's radiation. The film presentation was very successful in getting the attention of my fellow Air Intelligence School classmates as we began our first day of the Nuclear Warfare study segment of our twenty-eight-week air intelligence course.

The previous week's study block had consisted of a week of repugnant briefings and videos detailing the effects of chemical and biological warfare. Through briefings and photographic evidence, we learned about the effectiveness and consequences of the offensive use chemical warfare products such as nerve agents, blistering agents, respiratory agents and cyanides along with data on the use of biological warfare agents such as anthrax, botulism, plague, and smallpox.

We had learned how a pound of LSD added to the water supply of New York City at its source could incapacitate the entire population of the city for two days, making it defenseless from any would-be attacker. Following that segment, we were shown the before-and-after film footage of a dozen hapless U.S. Army "volunteers" tripping out on LSD while trying to negotiate an obstacle course. Yes, this was the 1960s and the chemists and psychiatrists were busy fulfilling their government grants to develop more effective Cold War weapons. As it turned out, the insidious weaponizing of LSD has backfired and incapacitated millions of Americans since its development, leaving them violent or unpredictable, harming themselves and others.

Even with that previous week's subject matter, my classmates and I were still not fully prepared for an immersion into nuclear warfare and what our participation might be in carrying out the deployment of the most intensely deadly weapon of modern warfare. The classroom was filled with a palpable discomfort as we began this next course of study.

In general we learned that, even on the smallest scale, any nuclear conflict would be catastrophic. We came to understand the severity of devastation that would ensue from escalation of combat forces into the level of nuclear warfare. This included projections as to the number people in a specified area who would die from blast damage, fallout radiation, and subsequent starvation during the cold weather conditions of the following winter. The possibility of nuclear conflict was the strongest and most dominant factor in international politics and U.S. policy ever since the beginning of the Cold War.

In addition to the tens of millions of deaths that would be incurred during the days and weeks following any attack and counter-attack in a nuclear conflict zone such as Western and Central Europe, there would probably be further millions (perhaps hundreds of millions) of deaths from body disintegration resulting from radiation in the ensuing months or years. This goes far beyond the concept of disabling the occupants of a major city with LSD.

The only measurable historical reference for the amount of nuclear devastation potential for an urban setting had been the recorded results of the nuclear bomb that was dropped on Hiroshima in August 1945, with a blast yield of fifteen kilotons (a force equivalent to fifteen thousand tons of TNT).

At the moment of its detonation, some seventy thousand people died as a result of the initial blast and its heat and radiation effects. Because of the lingering effects of radioactive fallout and other after-effects, the Hiroshima death toll was probably greater than one hundred thousand by the end of 1945. It had been estimated that the five-year loss of life may have reached or even exceeded two hundred thousand, as cancer and other long-term effects took their tolls.

We learned that, in addition to the enormous economic and facilities destruction that would be caused by the actual nuclear explosions, there would be some years during which the surrounding economies would decline even further. There was no way to estimate the degree to which industrial and agricultural production might collapse in the areas attacked.

And, of course, there would be a high probability of significant long-term and widespread ecological damage. As I saw it, this was going way beyond an inconvenient truth and had entered into the realm of unthinkable and immeasurable consequences.

The long-term effects from fallout of a variety of radioactive substances also had to be taken into consideration. This included strontium-90, an isotope produced by nuclear fission. Once airborne after the blast, it would settle into the vegetation and water supplies over the battle area and other areas downwind from the blasts. When ingested by humans and other living creatures, strontium-90 is deposited in bones and bone marrow, with some remaining in blood and soft tissues. Its presence in bones had been determined to cause bone cancer, cancer of nearby tissues and leukemia.

Studies had shown that children born in St. Louis, Missouri, in 1963 had levels of strontium-90 in their baby teeth that was fifty times higher than those found in children born there in 1950, before the commencement of large-scale atomic testing at the Nevada Test Site located northwest of Las Vegas, Nevada. So, testing of nuclear weapons sixteen hundred miles to the west of St. Louis had had an enormous effect on these young lives. What level of contamination would an actual nuclear conflict bring to the Earth's atmosphere?

I was reminded of T.S. Eliot's 1925 poem "The Hollow Men" despairingly foreshadowing the fate of the world after World War I: "This is the way the world ends, not with a bang but a whimper." In modern times, after the initial blasts of thousands of nuclear weapons, would widespread nuclear contamination sicken and eventually exterminate most of the life forms on our planet?

After our instruction in the magnitude and consequences of nuclear warfare, we were then introduced to the military technical factors affecting aircraft and airfields. This was the connection to our intelligence study of the subject. To understand how to employ nuclear detonations in warfare, we learned that most initial damage comes from the explosive blast. The shock wave of air radiates outward, producing sudden changes in air pressure that can crush objects, and these are accompanied by high winds that can knock objects down. In general, large buildings are destroyed by the change in air pressure, while people and objects such as trees and utility poles along with residential and commercial structures would be destroyed by the wind. Duck and cover was obviously never an option.

Besides the devastating weapon effects of a nuclear blast of any magnitude on an enemy military facility, what else does an Air Intelligence officer need to know about nuclear blasts? Here's what we were taught about our role in nuclear warfare and how we would apply what we had learned.

When a nuclear weapon is detonated on or near the Earth's surface, the blast digs out a large crater. Some of the material that had been in the crater is deposited on the rim of the crater and the rest mushrooms up into the air. Therefore, if an attacking aircraft were to target an airfield using nuclear weapons, someone would have to determine how many and what size bombs and where they needed to be dropped to prevent responding aircraft taking off from the runway.

As it turned out, that calculation was a function of an Air Intelligence officer! I began to realize that, even among Air Force officers, this was the military and someone was going to be assigned to latrine duty; this was the spiritual and emotional version of that lowly function.

As a practical exercise in this segment, each class member was handed a Nuclear Weapon Effects Calculator issued by the Defense Nuclear Agency. (An illustration of an actual calculator is provided in the Illustrations section at the front of this book.) This was an analog computing device with a four-inch-diameter plastic wheel printed with variable slide calculations that provided the blast results of crater depth and crater radius, as well as air blast dynamic pressure and the overpressure caused by a shock wave over and above normal atmospheric pressure. The device user, in the classroom the Air Intelligence Officer in training, would provide data input of weapon force amount in kilotons or megatons (how forceful an explosion), selecting a choice of impact onto the targeted ground surface: either hard rock, dry soft rock, wet soil rock, or wet soil.

We were given a variety of actual aircraft runway specifications from World War II photo reconnaissance missions, including complex, multiple-runway layouts. We then input the data into our calculators and produced supposedly accurate calculations of the number of blasts on the runways that would be required to guarantee that no aircraft could take off in a counter-attack. After practicing with this device for two days, I found that I could pretty much look at any runway configuration from the air reconnaissance photos and immediately estimate the number and placement of hits to eradicate the response capability of any aircraft assigned to take off from that field.

Because some modern fighter aircraft (not including those with vertical take-off and landing ability) do not require a very long runway, the quantity of nuclear weapons needed to nullify the threat was enormous. I realized that most major military airfields with multiple runways would be targeted with about twenty nuclear blasts, taking out its aircraft counter-attack capability as well as wiping out all military and civilian facilities and life forms in a cataclysmic series of shock waves. The Effects Calculator was providing sizes and numbers of weapons that would ensure massive overkill and unnecessary widespread devastation in the areas surrounding the target. We had now been informed of the consequences of our possible participation in nuclear warfare and how we would direct the bombing missions. This was far from my expectation of gathering passive intelligence in a secure room protected from an active combat zone.

By the end of our Nuclear Warfare segment of study, every member of my Air Intelligence class – men, women and Marines – had fallen ill with flu symptoms that had apparently not touched any other officers or enlisted staff on the air base. Given a weekend to recover, we were all back in the classroom, ready to move on to the next subject. As if it never happened, the Nuclear Warfare study segment was never mentioned during any subsequent training weeks. But I was never able to dismiss from thought my ability to view an airfield, military or civilian, and then calculate its destruction and the knowledge of the consequent horror of nuclear war.

Now, what could this have to do with an Intelligence Watch Officer's job holed up under a mountain? Remember, the Bunker was the Command Center for Western Europe, and who would be more likely to survive an attack and direct a retaliation with the release of nuclear weapons?

A later Officer Performance Report stated more clearly than the first report mentioned earlier as to what my involvement in nuclear warfare would be: "… he is one of a small group of selected individuals responsible for the immediate handling and processing of highly sensitive Emergency Actions messages and codeword security/authentication and release procedures. His knowledge and responsiveness in the accomplishment of this function is considered outstanding and makes him a valuable member of the two-man positive control concept."

To put that into more understandable language, the Intelligence Watch Officer and the Sector Controller on duty at the SOC constituted the two-man nuclear weapons release authentication team for U.S. forces in Europe. Simulated drills of the procedure were required frequently to ensure that there were no hesitations or errors. "White" messages, of course, were only drills that simulated a notification from the President of the United States ordering the release of nuclear weapons as determined by whatever operations plan that had been authorized. A "red" message prefix meant the real thing.

At the time of my service, a special military officer accompanied the U.S. President wherever he went. He carried a nondescript briefcase nicknamed "the football." This briefcase contained the secret codes that were updated daily in order to launch a nuclear attack along with the list of targets and attack scenarios. To launch an attack, the President would need to confirm his identity using a code printed on a plastic card nicknamed "the biscuit," which the President was required to have in his possession at all times. "The football" and "the biscuit" were titles that had apparently followed the superficial and non-threatening nicknames that had been traditionally attributed to weapons of mass destruction since "Little Boy" was dropped on Hiroshima, followed by the "Fat Man" that was dropped on Nagasaki three days later, both named after film characters from the 1940s.

My participation in the simulation drills in the Bunker began with the receipt of an Emergency Broadcast Message on the operations room public address system, at which point the Sector Controller would vacate his command desk and enter the Intelligence booth, closing the pocket door behind him.

My first action in the drill sequence was to lock the pocket door behind the Sector Controller and commence opening the combination padlock that secured a steel bar that slid into two brackets welded onto the exterior of the steel two-drawer filing cabinet safe. This bar prevented either drawer from being opened. As the IWO on duty, I had the combination for the padlock and the Sector Controller had the combination for the safe's built-in combination lock. The top half of the safe and its drawer were painted white; the bottom half and its drawer were painted red. Of course, white was for exercises and red was for the real thing.

In the drill, I would unlock the padlock and draw up and out the steel bar fastener that had been held in place by the brackets welded to the safe, enabling the Sector Controller to then bend over to tumble the safe's built-in combination lock. When both locks had been opened, either the top white drawer or the bottom red drawer could be slid open, allowing access to the vinyl code envelopes.

Of course, all messages we had received were prefaced with "white." Inside the drawer was a collection of three-by-five-inch vinyl envelopes (our versions of the "biscuit"). The envelope to be selected contained the currently active release codes that coincided with the date of the Emergency Broadcast Message. I would cut open the vinyl envelope with scissors and the release codes would be displayed. The Sector Controller and I would each confirm that the codes on the broadcast were correct. These were the codes that authorized the release of nuclear weapons in Europe under the command of SOC III.

After drilling the procedure of authentication and release for many months, and having become proficient at the simulation of these orders, I began to contemplate the full consequences of the action I had been prepared to carry out. On receipt of a "red" message, I would be forwarding orders to implement a plan to engage Warsaw Pact aircraft or incoming missiles with our nuclear-equipped aircraft or surface-to-air missiles, or both.

I had determined early on in my military training that I would not hesitate to defend my life, the lives of my family members, fellow members of the U.S. armed forces and harmless citizens. I had been sufficiently trained in marksmanship with an M-16 rifle and a .38-caliber pistol and I was prepared and willing to defend human life as necessary.

However, the prospect of ordering nuclear armed forces to engage in an enemy air attack over Central and Western Europe extended beyond my commitment to self-defense into a much more extreme response level to external threats. On this post, I had been regularly practicing compliance with orders to release nuclear weapons that would create widespread destruction and the loss of life of countless non-participants in a military action of global magnitude.

I could not help but envision an aerial warfare above the NATO concentration of bases and weaponry in the defensive belt in West Germany, resulting in the destruction of the surrounding areas of Western and Central Europe and the contamination of much of the world.

The U.S. policy on our response to nuclear weapons deployed against the U.S. or its allies had been made quite clear to me and the rest of the world during what became known as the Cuban Missile Crisis of 1962. At that time, U.S. President John F. Kennedy had declared to Soviet Premier Nikita Khrushchev that the United States would not permit offensive weapons to be delivered to Cuba, located less than a hundred miles off the southern coast of Florida. He demanded that the Soviets dismantle the missile bases that had been built in Cuba and that all offensive weapons there had to be returned to the Soviet Union.

To publicize this threat, President Kennedy went on national television informing the American public of the developments in Cuba, his decision to implement a "quarantine" of Cuba and the potential military consequences if the crisis continued to escalate. Kennedy's message strongly and clearly stated, "It shall be the policy of this nation to regard any nuclear missile launched from Cuba against any nation in the Western Hemisphere as an attack by the Soviet Union on the United States, requiring a full retaliatory response upon the Soviet Union."

With this, a military readiness status of DEFCON 3 (a Defense Readiness Condition that made the Air Force ready to mobilize in fifteen minutes) was declared, as U.S. naval forces began implementation of the quarantine on shipments into Cuba and plans were moved forward for a U.S. military strike on Cuba.

With Soviet and U.S. naval forces swarming around the island of Cuba at heightened states of alert, the two superpowers came closer to a nuclear conflict than at any previous time during the Cold War. How close they came to all-out nuclear war was revealed forty years after the crisis with an announcement by the U.S. National Security Archive of George Washington University in Washington, D.C. The unthinkable had been about to happen.

Outside of direct control and communication from the White House or the Kremlin, the U.S. Navy had been dropping simulated depth charges using hand grenades near a Soviet Navy submarine trying to force it to surface, unaware that the sub was carrying nuclear weapons. The Soviet naval officers on board the sub had lost radio contact with Moscow. They concluded from the apparent depth charge attack that World War III had begun, with two of the officers agreeing to "blast the warships out of the water" with their nuclear torpedoes, which would have started the nuclear conflict and defied Kennedy's threat of nuclear retaliation.

In accord with Soviet launch protocols, unanimous consent of all three officers on board was required to release the nuclear weapons. Vasilli Arkhipov, second-in-command of the submarine, refused to agree with his captain's order to the launch nuclear torpedoes against the U.S. warships in its vicinity.

Arkhipov argued against the launch, pointing out that they should first confirm that a state of war actually existed before releasing nuclear weapons, and he eventually convinced the captain to not only hold off on the attack, but even to risk destruction by surfacing the submarine to establish radio contact. The Soviet submarine emerged from the waves amid its pursuers without incident. After resuming communications with the Soviet Union and learning that the war had not commenced, the sub's captain headed his vessel for home.

The National Security Archive announcement in 2002 stated clearly that Arkhipov had "saved the world." The extraordinary and sensible actions of this hero of the Cold War enabled us to continue our lives in relative calm by avoiding a global catastrophe. Thank you for your outstanding contribution to mankind, Vasilli Arkhipov!

Twenty years after the first nuclear bomb was detonated in July 1945, Robert Oppenheimer, the scientific director of the project that developed the atom bomb, described the initial reactions of the observers: "We knew the world would not be the same. A few people laughed.... A few people cried.... Most people were silent. I remembered the line from the Hindu scripture that says, 'Now I am become death, the destroyer of worlds.' I suppose we all thought that, one way or another."

Even without the knowledge of Oppenheimer's misgivings, with all of the knowledge I had obtained in my Nuclear Warfare study, I had come to the same conclusion that I could never take actions that would put nuclear warfare into effect and become a destroyer of worlds.

After drilling the procedure for release authentication about ten times, I had resolved to devise a scenario that would remove me from participation in an act that would be so harmful to many millions of human lives. I stood alone in the booth on several occasions and mentally walked myself through the following scenario.

On receipt of an actual "red" Emergency message, I would immediately ensure that the release order was in accord with current intelligence regarding existing or impending hostilities. If the release order was not consistent with verifiable data and there was no indication of threatened hostilities, I would attempt to convince the Sector Controller that the order needed to be queried for further confirmation once we had authenticated the code. If he still insisted on following through on the release order, despite the evidence I presented, I would implement a simple plan.

It merely entailed the action of pulling out the safe's steel bar, striking the other two-man team member (the Sector Controller) unconscious with the bar and returning the bar and the padlock to their locked positions. Then, I'd be off to the parking lot, down the mountain road to pick up Chris at our room or at her hospital ward. I would inform her of what had occurred, and we would head south on a high-speed road trip to Switzerland where I would most likely be arrested at some later date. And I would be free from having contributed to the loathsome act of mass destruction that would have haunted me forever.

Through correct estimation of situations and incidents on my watch and with some good fortune, I never had to enact any part of this plan!

DECISIONS HAVE BEEN MADE

AT THE TIME THAT I had been struggling with my responsibilities as a nuclear release officer, Chris was trying to make the best of her duties as a nurse at the Army hospital attending soldiers who had been evacuated there from Vietnam. She had mentioned to me previously that she had enlisted into the Army Nurse Corps to fulfill her purpose of saving lives, that she had even requested specifically an assignment in Vietnam so she could nurse our soldiers in the combat zone. This request had been denied due to her young age of nineteen and her lack of military nursing experience. That had been the reason for her assignment to Germany.

I first learned of her personal conflict when she arrived home early from her day shift in mid-afternoon while I was getting ready for a swing shift. She briskly entered our room in her nurse whites and announced to me that she had just walked off her shift on the hospital ward while she was pouring medications for wounded soldiers. She had suddenly understood that she had not merely been nursing combat victims, but that, in the larger sense, she was patching up these men so they could return to battle to kill other men, and that they would then later return for more medical care to get patched up to go out again to kill more men.

I had understood what she had come to realize about her work and told her so. I saw the consequences of this act of defiance to her life and mine. I asked her if she was prepared to go to prison for five years for deserting her post in a time of war. Without hesitation, she set her white nurse's cap back on her head, walked quickly down the hill to the hospital and returned to her nurse's station. Her reluctance to aid the soldiers had been outweighed by the personal consequences she might have to endure. She had made the right decision for herself, and for us, and she continued in service until her period of enlistment was fulfilled a year later.

* * *

Occasionally, Chris and I were able to coordinate her nursing schedule with my watch schedule so that we could share time off for two or three days, an opportunity for rest and relaxation away from the Bunker and the hospital. In March of 1968, we headed out on a trip on an unusually sunny and warm time for our locale. We had set our sights on Munich which was about three hundred miles away from our quarters and less than a three-hour drive in the Porsche on the autobahn. It was an exhilarating high-speed drive that pushed our concerns about the Cold War and Vietnam behind us, with a soundtrack provided by Radio Veronica blaring on the Blaupunkt car radio system.

Still feeling somewhat agitated about my decision regarding carrying out nuclear release orders, I had also been looking ahead as to what part I might play in life after I had completed my military service in another two years. Before my life had been so rudely interrupted by my draft notice,

I had had vague plans of pursuing a career in marketing and advertising. I had studied what was called Mass Media Studies in college and found it be an engrossing and probably a lucrative, fun and creative way to make a living. I had devoured books such as Marshall McLuhan's *Understanding Media* and spent many pleasurable hours in library research for my term paper on "The Social Influences of Films of the 1940s," putting to good use my late-night TV viewing.

I had also had in mind a notion to pursue politics on a state level to fulfill my desire to contribute to and enhance the world around me that was obviously in need of some improvement. Through my father, I already had some strong connections to the political and business leaders in my state. So, it had occurred to me that, if I could be successful at marketing, I might then be able to turn that knowledge into a success in the political arena.

That plan had never been more than some indefinite thoughts that I had occasionally bounced around in my head while I fulfilled these obligations in the military.

Then, on this high-speed road trip to Munich, somewhere between a hundred and ten and a hundred and twenty miles per hour, I experienced an awakening. Those plans and dreams, along with the knowledge I had obtained in Intelligence School and my real-world participation in the Cold War had collided with an admonition best summarized by e. e. cummings that I had to be myself in a "world which was doing its best day and night to make me like everybody else." These thoughts all came together as a single conclusion that clearly proclaimed to me: "I couldn't go back," and that I would have to become who I really was and swerve away from a life that had been aligned with acceptance and approval in a world that I could clearly see was not quite right.

This meant that I would no longer pursue a career in advertising or one in politics that I now considered would be diminishing myself by setting my sights on attaining wealth and influence when we were caught in a world of conflicts, deceptions and human suffering. I had also understood that there were not yet any political or social systems that could directly improve the lot of man beyond the cycles of destruction that had been repeated throughout history. It was time for me to discover who I really was and what I was willing to do with my life and then find ways to contribute to a better world.

* * *

With my attention fully back on the road, we were less than twenty miles outside Munich when I noticed an exit sign marked "Dachau." This was very unexpected, and my curiosity was immediately aroused, connecting this journey with my studies of German history. Was there any greater symbol of human conflict and suffering than this Nazi concentration camp?

I exited the autobahn and drove directly into the village of Dachau. Both Chris and I scanned each side of the main street looking for any signage directing us to the former concentration camp but soon found we were heading out of the small village onto a dirt road that led into a lonely forest. The road ended abruptly in a quiet wooded area with a stone marker that stated in German and in English "GRAVE OF THOUSANDS UNKNOWN." We were amazed to have discovered what appeared to be the only memorial to the thousands of victims from the Dachau concentration camp. We had been expecting to find the actual restored camp, not a stone marker that essentially rested on the ground in denial of the true events in the life of this village.

But I had recalled reading recently that the camp at Dachau had been provided newly refurbished buildings and a memorial befitting the magnitude of this infamous human tragedy. Determined to find the camp, we headed back through the village, driving slowly, scanning left and right until we saw a group of one-story buildings behind several village residences on our left. Finally, we came upon the entrance to the camp with its rusted iron gates and blocky rusted letters that read ARBEIT MACHT FREI (work sets you free). My assumption that the camp would have been placed away from the village and out of sight had been incorrect; it had been located just behind the back yards of the village houses all along!

Since we were the only visitors to this new facility, we decided to take an unguided walking tour through the museum. The walls and room partitions of the museum vividly depicted the story with floor-to-ceiling black and white photos taken by American soldiers who had first encountered the inmates in the liberation of the camp in 1945. Many of the photos clearly displayed the horrific conditions of the Dachau inmates. It almost seemed impolite to stare at the personal mistreatment and degradation that these people had suffered.

The captions on the photos in English and German instructed us that the camp had been set up for political prisoners in 1933 and had served as a model for later concentration camps and as a "school of violence" for the SS men who commanded it. The first major segregation of old, sick, and weak prisoners by the medical commission had been established in 1941. This "special treatment" program, also referred to as Aktion T4, set apart Jewish prisoners as a group. A hundred or more inmates at Dachau were chosen once or twice a week, and then were moved into the prisoners' baths. The baths at Dachau had been restored and we had assumed these were the gas chambers we had learned about in our historical studies about concentration camps.

But what actually had occurred was that many of the prisoners who had not died from starvation and neglect at the camp had been crowded into two collection buses each week. They were then transported to Hartheim Castle, near Linz, Austria, a hundred and fifty miles away and more than a three-hour drive from Dachau and west of Munich.

The Hartheim Castle Euthanasia Center had been established under the medical direction of Dr. Rudolf Lonauer, a psychiatrist from Linz. He was also the medical director of the District Sanatorium and Nursing Home in Linz, which served as a holding station for victims on their way to Hartheim. He was personally responsible for the deaths of thousands of victims, determining their causes of death and keeping patient records. In 1945, an hour before the arrival of the U.S. Army, he murdered his wife and two young daughters and then committed suicide.

His deputy medical director was Dr. Georg Renno, former assistant to psychiatrist Hermann Paul Nitsche, the acknowledged expert in developing unobtrusive methods of killing using medicine. In 1945, Renno fled from apprehension after the war and assumed an alias working for Schering, a German pharmaceutical company that introduced the first birth control pill in the European market in 1961. The company later diversified its product line to include a broad spectrum of pharmaceuticals. These included X-ray contrast media, industrial chemicals and psycho-pharmaceuticals, with the latter most likely drawing intense interest and research from Dr. Renno.

He was later brought to trial and released without being convicted due to his "physical ailments," which obviously never contributed to a short life. Thirty years after his release, in 1997, at the age of ninety, he stated, "I have a calm conscience. I do not feel guilty.... After seeing how the people died, I have to say it was no pain for them,... It was a redemption."

As the "spiritual" leader of the many advocates of psychiatric solutions based on racial hygiene in Germany, other European countries and the U.S., Dr. Nitsche had proposed public health measures directed at strengthening the "national body" by eliminating biologically threatening genes from the population. Surgical sterilizations and elimination through murder were the solutions to purify the gene pool that had been envisioned as undergoing a "national death" in Germany. As early as 1939, he was involved in planning the murder of patients. By 1941, he ran the medical side of Aktion T4, campaigning heavily for reorganizing psychiatry according to the principle of "healing and annihilation."

Arrested in 1945, he was condemned to death for crimes against humanity for killing over one thousand people. He attempted to justify his actions, stating they were intended to free the sick from pain. A guillotine freed him from his pain in 1948 in Dresden.

In the twelve years of its existence, more than two hundred thousand people from all over Europe were imprisoned at Dachau and in its numerous subsidiary camps. More than forty-one thousand of those prisoners had been murdered by shipping them to Hartheim Castle for psychiatric evaluation and extermination.

Well, that was enough of those horror stories and certainly sufficient confirmation that it was time for me to discover what I was willing to do with my life and find ways to contribute to a better world.

We were, after all, in Munich to enjoy a two-day getaway for rest and relaxation in that charming city, distancing ourselves from the daily reminders of war, political tensions and man's inhumanity to man.

Once settled into our small hotel room, we made the obligatory visit to the Hofbräuhaus beer hall in the center of town. With large glass steins of the local brew, we took in the beer hall's four-piece brass and accordion oompah band playing its foot-stomping, thigh-slapping German folk tunes. Not exactly the music we were into in the late 1960s, but a sight to behold.

Then we went off across the street to our final act of tourism in Munich to take in the Glockenspiele clock tower chimes with its show of musical bells and dancing figures. These well-orchestrated tourist attractions were amusing and had provided some pleasant distractions and a relief from the great sadness we had experienced witnessing Dachau's compelling display. And those steins of high-alcohol-content German beer had eased us into a relaxed and restful night under the hotel bed's immense down comforter. We had achieved our hoped-for separation from the Cold War and wounded combatants.

PUSHING SOME BUTTONS

I'VE DESCRIBED SOME OF THE significant events on the Intelligence Watch post during that period earlier in this story. But the most significant event of my tour in Germany occurred at the end of November, 1968. On what was a day before a Thanksgiving Day being celebrated in the U.S. but not in Germany and not even at our BOQ, Lieutenant Christine Cooke and Lieutenant Bruce Rigney were married in a German civil ceremony conducted by the Officiating Registrar at the Birkenfeld Town Hall.

In accordance with German law, we had had to register our request for a marriage license as American citizens in Germany by driving north for more than two hours to Cologne and formally requesting marriage banns two weeks prior to the marriage. These announcements of our intention to marry were posted in the local church in Birkenfeld. This procedure gave community members a chance to object to the marriage.

It also gave Chris some time to put together a unique wedding outfit consisting of dark blue velvet gaucho pants, a matching gold-trimmed velvet vest and a dark blue velvet floppy-brimmed hat, all mail-ordered from the U.S. A few days before the appointed date, Chris was still looking for black, knee-high boots to complete the look. There were none to be found in the Hunsrück – not a fashion center at that time. So, we headed south for an hour to the French border at Saarbrücken. Relying on the French as a fashion source, we were not disappointed when we found the right boots and in her size.

Many months had passed since our trip to Munich. With our friend Andy having been shipped off to Vietnam and Jeannine returning to the U.S., we selected two Army enlisted friends as witnesses to the ceremony. Chris was adorable in her wedding outfit. The ceremony was conducted in heavily accented Hunsrück German with Chris and I affirming "Ja" each time the Registrar looked at us expectantly. We couldn't imagine "Nein" being a proper answer in a marriage ceremony, and we were only completely certain that we had passed this oral examination when the Registrar had signed and stamped our marriage license certificate, all in German of course. As a word of advice to anyone anxious about wedding ceremony jitters, just have it conducted in a language you don't quite get the meaning of – a walk in the park.

As a married couple, we were now eligible to apply for a supplemental income payment that would allow us to live on the German economy. We found a house overlooking a farm village called Schwollen located less than six miles away from the Bunker. Yes, we loved the location and the name, which translated to "swelled up" in English! It has never ceased to make us smile whenever we mention our first home. The two-story hillside house overlooked a broad valley blanketed with farm fields crossed by a single village road with several farmhouses grouped together surrounding the obligatory village gasthaus.

The house had three bedrooms, a kitchen, a living room and a bath. All the rooms were furnished and it rented for less than the Air Force's allowance for a rental unit on the economy. On first viewing, there was no need to look further. It was spacious and within our budget.

After being shown the heating system, I did have second thoughts: it was a downstairs coal furnace in a coal room with a chute from outside that supplied the coal. I could live with that, even though I had only experienced oil and gas heating systems in the U.S. Of course, in the coldest months of winter, my daily routine now consisted of stumbling out of bed in the early morning, down to the first floor to stoke the furnace! This was a new house in the twentieth century; like so many of my experiences in the this mountain range, I felt that I had dropped back a half century or more.

The house in Schwollen provided a private and peaceful home where Chris was able to show off her cooking and homemaking skills and where we could entertain guests. Since we had no nearby neighbors and could roll down the sound-dampening wooden window shutters, we were able to put our stereo system to good use at some remarkable decibel levels.

Having settled into a period of domestic comfort, we continued to hear more about the protests against the Vietnam War from friends in the military and in articles in magazine and other news sources, even some references to it in the military newspaper *The Stars and Stripes*. To learn more about what was happening in the U.S., we had mailed away for subscriptions to *The Village Voice* in New York and *The Berkeley Barb* in San Francisco. These newspapers provided us with timely although somewhat slanted news. The popular phrase of the era expressing distrust of the system "Don't trust anyone over thirty" comes to mind. We learned what was happening in the U.S. concerning the war protests and racial unrest, cultural opinions and interests that were changing America and were now extending into Europe.

With access to non-mainstream publications and the pirate station Radio Veronica, we had abundant recommendations about the latest music that we searched out in local record stores. We were able to keep track of the latest tunes from The Beatles, The Rolling Stones, The Doors, Jefferson Airplane, Buffalo Springfield and Steppenwolf, among many others. And we were introduced to 1960's classic protest songs such as "Eve of Destruction," "Draft Dodger Rag," "I-Feel-Like-I'm-Fixin'-to-Die Rag," "Bad Moon Rising," and many others, not to be outdone by "War, What Is It Good For, Huh!?"

Three months later, in February 1969, Chris completed her two-year active duty commitment as a First Lieutenant in the Army Nurse Corps and returned to the U.S. to be honorably discharged from service. After a short visit home with her parents, she returned to me as my civilian wife, technically as my military "dependent." At that time, there was no term used in the military to describe a wife who was smart, self-determined, often assertive and very *in*dependent. Before getting married, I had been advised in several conversations with senior officers that wives should be looked upon as needing to be supportive and useful and to be treated with tolerance, as needed. I knew that this wife of mine needed to be as free as the Rolling Stones' Ruby Tuesday, not chained to a life "where nothing's gained, and nothing's lost."

As part of Chris' role in the home, she would often drop me off at the Bunker for my shift and then drive down to Birkenfeld Air Station to purchase food and household basics. She would also stop off to pick up our mail at the Air Station post office where we would receive letters from family and friends, publications and a few catalogs from which Chris was able to purchase clothing and other items not available in Germany.

By the end of May 1969, I had served nearly two years on the Intelligence Watch Officer post. My Officer Performance Reports were even more glowing than all earlier reports. Under the heading of Facts and Other Achievements, my new senior officer, Captain Lenahan, reported that, "Lt. Rigney is one of the most intelligent young officers that I have ever encountered. This coupled with his cheerfulness and cooperative manner have made him a valuable asset to this unit." He went on to report that, "His personal credo is such that it allows for nothing less than the best.... developing procedure aids that have been incorporated into the daily operation of the Intelligence Watch position.... He has repeatedly demonstrated exceptional competence and skill while serving in Command Post exercises, always accomplishing all actions in an efficient and timely manner." Pretty good recommendation, huh?

But wait, there's more! Before receiving that glowing recommendation, I had been informed that my seniors had submitted my name and accomplishments as the local candidate for the award of Air Force Intelligence Officer of the Year for Europe.

Then two things happened. The Sector Operations Center received a new commander for the detachment, a Colonel Babb. On meeting him, I saw that this was an arrogant and domineering senior officer and that he was not going to make life easy under his command. As the new man on the job, and without the security clearance level required for this command, he exhibited an overly confident and abrasive attitude toward the Intelligence Watch Officer staff.

Then Chris, my Ruby Tuesday "unchained" as it were, showed up at the Air Station post office one morning wearing her floppy broad-brimmed hat and her flower-print jeans – very now and attractive. And prominently displayed on her olive-drab Army fatigue jacket, she wore a one-and-a-half-inch-diameter pin-on button.

In bright colors it stated, "I AM ASHAMED OF WHAT MY COUNTRY IS DOING IN VIETNAM." Chris had shown me the button before she wore it and I had expressed my support of the button's sentiment, but it did occur to me that I was about to see a "bad moon a-rising and some trouble on the way."

Sure enough, two days after Chris' visit to the post office, Lt. Colonel Forsythe, not yet fully replaced as the commander of the SOC detachment, met with me privately in the IWO booth. He regretted to inform me that the new commander had ordered that I be removed from post and placed under investigation for subversion. A report had been received about my wife's button and the fact that we were receiving "underground" publications at our mailbox. So much for freedom of expression and thought.

I was immediately removed from post and assigned as the officer in charge of managing the Birkenfeld Air Station sports equipment office, logging out the baseballs, bats and gloves for use at the station's ball field. I was also put in charge of arranging the fireworks display and refreshments for the upcoming Fourth of July picnic and celebration. And there went any prospect for that award as Intelligence Officer of the Year. Not that important, but always good to be validated for a job well done.

I had assured Chris that I had broken no rules and that I could not be prosecuted in the absence of any evidence of wrongdoing on my part. We would just have to ride this out and make it work for us. Really, just another "situation normal, all fouled up."

The investigation for subversion would be conducted to discover any actions I might have committed that were designed to undermine the strength or morale of my unit, presumably through a compromise of the classified data that had been entrusted to me. Certainly, I had never spoken a word to anyone about my job description or revealed any classified information. And I had never commented on the Vietnam War, despite two senior officers confiding to me on separate occasions that North Vietnam should be "nuked." I left each of those conversations with no response. In all of my communications, I had only stated that I "worked at the Bunker" to other servicemen and their spouses, and even to my wife.

A week into the investigation, I was ordered to meet with the local Office of Special Investigations (OSI) about fifty miles away from the Bunker in our unit's headquarters at Ramstein Air Force Base, less than an hour's drive down the mountain road. OSI is a law enforcement agency that investigates and "neutralizes serious criminal, terrorist, and espionage threats to personnel and resources of the U.S. Air Force." So, what had occurred here was that my wife's protest button had pushed someone's buttons, seemingly posing a serious threat to the Air Force, and I was about to be neutralized in some way.

I met the two OSI agents, both in dark civilian suits, white shirts and dark ties in their front office, and they immediately led me to an interior back office. This was a seven-foot by seven-foot, windowless, sound-proofed interview space that could fit only a small desk between the interviewee and the two agents sitting between the desk and the door, obviously blocking any attempted escape or violent behavior.

The interview consisted of questions about my opinions of the Vietnam War, the publications I was receiving, any books I was reading and any connections to groups that intended to overthrow the government. I was handed a list of "subversive" groups and individuals that I might be connected with and I responded in the negative to them all as I scanned through the list. These included war protest organizations, Socialist and Communist groups as well as human rights groups, religious leaders and popular new religious groups.

The agents took turns in their questioning, with one quickly following the other, an obvious attempt to throw me off guard. I was handling this well. My responses were rapid, appropriate and apparently favorably received. I was on my game! I had expected them to use a good-cop/bad-cop approach, but the agents and I were getting along quite well.

When asked about my opinions on the Vietnam War, I merely espoused what both the Republicans and Democrats had been proposing in the political debates of the 1968 national election: A gradual withdrawal of U.S. forces from Vietnam and a negotiation for peace between the North and South. I was questioned about books I had recently read, any current religious or political affiliations, and what I planned to do when I had completed my service commitment.

At this point in the interview, I realized that I had just been handed an opportunity to obtain what I had hoped to achieve: dismissal of all charges, an escape from the wrath of my new commander and, finally, a reprieve from the dreadful prospect of receiving and executing an order to release nuclear weapons. I just needed to put myself in control of the situation.

My response to the agents about my possible future employment scenario included that I might be working with some friends of my father who had supported the winning campaign for the former governor of my home state, John Chafee of Rhode Island. Under the new Nixon administration, Chafee happened to be the newly appointed Secretary of the Navy. Both agents went silent, looked to each other, folded up their papers and thanked me for my time.

There were no further repercussions from the button incident except, of course, from Colonel Babb who took exception from my rave Performance Review by stating, "I concur except.… His judgment as to what is acceptable conduct for himself and his dependents, and his choice of associates, has embarrassed this command and the USAF during this reporting period."

His senior, Colonel Weart, Deputy Chief of Staff at Seventeenth Air Force headquarters, took exception to Babb's exception and stated, "I am aware of the incident referred to by the additional endorsing official and do not consider this to be representative of Lt. Rigney's conduct." Obviously, Colonel Weart had placed a greater value on competence and willingness to get the job done than Colonel Babb, who never did obtain the security clearance to continue as the detachment commander at the Sector Operations Center.

After a successful Fourth of July celebration on the baseball field across the street from the Birkenfeld Air Station, including a large crowd of Germans and Americans in attendance enjoying plenty of burgers, hot dogs and not a single fireworks misfire, I was transferred to Ramstein Air Base to another top-secret intelligence officer position. My years on the Watch at the Bunker were over. I would receive no more orders, simulated or actual, for the release of nuclear weapons.

MY LAST ASSIGNMENT

AFTER THE FOURTH OF JULY celebration at Birkenfeld Air Station, I was given my written orders for transfer to Ramstein Air Force Base, forty-four miles down the mountain road. I had been assigned to the 26th Tactical Reconnaissance Wing as an Intelligence Officer in the Targets Branch. That was the action of directing aircraft to gather data using photos and other recording devices – no bombing!

Chris and I had packed up our household belongings at the house in Schwollen and departed there on the same day that the Air Force shipped these items to our new apartment in Ramstein. We had been moved into a convenient and comfortable apartment building for officers on the base, which featured many amenities including two bedrooms, a living room and a kitchen, all fully furnished. The base was adjacent to an active German city called Kaiserslautern, a large, autobahn-adjacent city with a population of nearly one hundred thousand that was still rebuilding and recovering from the destruction of Allied bombing in World War II. The air base also featured a fine restaurant and a mini-bowling alley with five-inch balls without finger holes!

The primary activity in the Targets Branch was the production of target folders for reconnaissance aircraft that might be sent out over hostile territory within the Warsaw Pact countries in the event of an impending future conflict. Target folders consisted of a flipbook of sequential topographical maps that a pilot would strap to his thigh to assist him in carrying out his designated flight plan. As he turned each page, the pilot was able to view the map segment that would show heading, altitude and turn points with heading adjustments to follow the required reconnaissance route.

The activity provided the opportunity to keep my mind and hands busy with calculations and problem-solving with target updates required on a continuous basis as new information became available on the routes. This work was challenging and interesting, somewhat similar in stress level to when I had worked as a machinist during summers to pay my college tuition. It certainly could not be compared to the stress and alarm of the Watch at the Bunker. We had a comfortable schedule with eight-hour days and one-hour lunch breaks, five days a week and no rotating late-night shifts. After several months of routine on this assignment, Chris and I were able to take our first vacation with a one-week trip to the Canary Islands.

Target folder preparation was conducted on the air base inside a secure, windowless vault of about twenty feet by twenty feet. An older career sergeant near his retirement taught me the procedures and standards for building the target folders, and we worked on target folder production together. The locked vault had a large central layout table surrounded with map cases. We sat at the table on stools that enabled us to move smoothly from standing to seated positions while unfolding, cutting and aligning the maps.

Early on in this assignment, I realized that I had finally attained what I had envisioned at the Air Force Recruiter's office in 1966 when I had selected Intelligence and Germany as my career and location preferences. It had taken nearly three years to arrive at the desired assignment, but I was now safely working in a comfortable, secure space, an actual vault, using my knowledge and skills for passive acquisition of intelligence data at the largest Air Force base in Germany. I had quickly become proficient with precision cut-and-paste techniques using scalpels from the base infirmary and rubber cement, and I was able to take pride in my productivity. Later in my life, this would come in handy when I became a graphic designer doing layouts for magazines.

My final two Officer Performance Reports in December and June 1970 stated that, "During the reporting period, Lt. Rigney was promoted to Captain.… His high degree of enthusiasm, knowledge and professionalism, and his ability to produce superior work under stress has quickly made him an essential member of the Branch. In the performance of his duties, he has exhibited versatility, imagination and mature judgment. …Captain Rigney is a person of superior intelligence, who has the rare ability to immediately grasp and comprehend problems, and select the best course of action to resolve the problem. His performance and unexcelled professional skill sets a high standard for those who work with him." Not bad for a subversive "embarrassment to the command and the U.S. Air Force"!

In October of 1970, Chris and I returned to the U.S. where I was officially, gratefully and honorably discharged from the U.S. Air Force. Not only had I dodged the bullet headed in my direction in 1966, but I had also avoided pulling any triggers, particularly that launch order for unleashing a nuclear catastrophe in Europe and defusing potential battle scenarios while on the Watch.

GETTING BETTER ALL THE TIME

IN MY PRESENT-DAY RESEARCH FOR this book in order to discover "Whatever happened to…?" I came across some pleasantly surprising developments, some of which are well known but should be acknowledged as circumstances that have now been favorably resolved. Some others are very positive developments that exceeded my expectations, leaving just one subject area that has yet defied a positive resolution.

The Vietnam War

With a new administration in Washington, the handwriting that was faintly written on the wall since before the start of the Vietnam War had finally been brought into stark focus and translated into political actions. The Nixon Administration adroitly and slowly maneuvered the U.S. away from the conflict in Vietnam, after using the unpopularity of the war to ensure the campaign withdrawal of Lyndon Johnson before the 1968 Presidential election, and thereby assuring the Nixon election to the Presidency.

In April of 1972, the last of about two million young men who had been drafted during the Vietnam era was enlisted into the U.S. Army, temporarily ending that period of forced induction into the military. Then in 1975, the U.S. Ambassador to South Vietnam and the Marines protecting him were evacuated from the roof of the U.S. Embassy famously photographed while ascending to a transport helicopter as they became the last group of American servicemen to depart Vietnam. This marked the end of the failed attempt to forcibly impose democracy in Southeast Asia and provided me with a tremendous relief from concerns about the perpetuation of my country's political and military deception and forceful intervention in Vietnam.

The Two Germanys United

In November 1989, the head of East Berlin's Communist Party announced that citizens of East Germany were free to cross the country's borders. East and West Berliners flocked to the wall chanting, "Open the gate!" and then flooded through the previously barricaded checkpoints along the wall.

More than two million people from East Berlin visited West Berlin in that first weekend with people on both sides using hammers and pickaxes to knock away chunks of the concrete wall. As I viewed television coverage of masses of jubilant Berliners assaulting the wall, I experienced a great relief from the emotional tension I had built up in my two years while on the watch over the Iron Curtain. Shortly afterward, cranes and bulldozers pulled down the wall and Berlin was united for the first time since 1945. The reunification of East and West Germany was made official in October 1990.

In March 1991, Soviet military commanders relinquished their control of the Warsaw Pact forces. A few months later, the Warsaw Pact met for the last time and officially acknowledged its dissolution. The end of the Cold War brought tremendous geopolitical and economic changes between the U.S., NATO, and the Soviet Union. The newly free Eastern and Central European countries had now left their Soviet legacies behind and some had even integrated into Western security forces and democratic structures.

The Börfink Bunker

With the Sector Operations Center located for a few years in the vicinity of Ramstein Air Base after 1969, an overhaul of the Börfink Bunker began in February 1976 to reconfigure it with updated electronics equipment and finally the Börfink Bunker was shut down in 2002.

More than a decade later, the Bunker would emerge as a new business enterprise in the Hunsrück. In 2015, a German data security provider, IT Vision Technology (ITVT), spent two years modifying the Bunker into a secure data storage facility designed to run with minimal dependency on the outside world. The underground server rooms deep beneath the ground now operated in a low-oxygen environment that greatly reduced the risk of fire damage, where even matches could not burn.

The facility had been made independent of the local power grid and used photovoltaic roof panels along with wind-generating power plants and local biodiesel fuel sources. Heat generated by the equipment at the Bunker is stored and distributed locally, benefitting the local community as well as its on-site technicians.

The extra security afforded by placing a data center free of the power grid in a nuclear-proof building was not merely a shrewd business opportunity. ITVT also serves NATO air forces as part of its customer base, with the Bunker once again providing security of another kind for the defense of Western Europe.

The Birkenfeld Air Station

In 1969, Birkenfeld Air Station was officially turned over to the Germans for use as an army transport facility for the next ten years. It again became an Air Force Support Group facility in 1979 and then a NATO facility in 1983, both in support of the Börfink Bunker. It finally closed in 1994 with the property transferred to the town of Birkenfeld. Current planning includes expansion for the existing Birkenfeld Hospital that shares a common property line.

At the front entrance to the former air station stands a two-foot-tall bronze plaque displaying the U.S. Air Force seal and inscribed with:

BIRKENFELD AIR STATION
1948-1969

For twenty-one years, an integral part of the United States Air Force and North Atlantic Treaty Organization, Allied Sector III. This site was the center of the Air Defense System for Western Germany.

This plaque is dedicated to the 4,359 Men and Women who were stationed here and their memories of friendships with each other and with the wonderful people of Birkenfeld and nearby towns.

Dedicated
June, 2007

The Neubrücke Army Hospital

In 1994, the U.S. Army's 98th General Hospital at Neubrücke was closed. The hospital's former property and buildings are now home to the Environmental Campus Birkenfeld (ECB), a branch of the Trier University of Applied Sciences. Currently there are more than twenty-five hundred students enrolled at the school with about sixty professors teaching Environmental Planning and Environmental Technology as well as Environmental Business and Environmental Law. The school is structured as a residential campus offering education, housing and employment all in one location, unusual in Germany. It is the only university in Germany that uses renewable energy sources to generate its heat.

As a university of applied sciences, students take part in research projects available on campus or travel to foreign countries to work on projects for two-week periods, engaged in activities such as developing renewable energy sources in places as diverse as Poland and China. There is a plan for future projects to be conducted in Brazil, with university students from the Hunsrück most likely reconnecting with nineteenth-century Hunsrücker emigrants.

There are eight residential structures that provide housing for nearly eight hundred students. Many of these students live in the now updated versions of our former BOQs. Just outside these residences, the school, perhaps unknowingly, displays some of its American heritage with an annual beach volleyball tournament on a court covered with imported beach sand. At this same location five decades ago, young American officers and nurses had thrown down towels on the lawn to "catch some rays" on the few sunny summer days in the Hunsrück.

Hoppstädten and Neubrücke

Also in 1994, a unique commercial venture was established on property near the former Army hospital and U.S. Army air base located adjacent to the villages of Hoppstädten and Neubrücke. More than two hundred mid-sized commercial enterprises from China have now settled into this segment of the Birkenfeld district. Nearly six hundred Chinese live together in the newly constructed Oak Garden district of Neubrücke.

The participating companies are primarily focused on the German market, but also on business ventures in other European countries. Each company operates as both an exporter and an importer. They include a wide range of commercial enterprises such as toys, textiles, food, mechanics and medical technology.

Approximately eighty Chinese children have attended kindergartens and schools in the area where they have learned German quickly and speak with the unique Hunsrücker dialect. The Chinese parents go to German clubs and some local Germans participate in Oak Garden dance clubs or tai chi classes. They celebrate at New Years' festivals together and take part in the local annual cultural festival.

This unique trading center has enjoyed great success with all the apartments in the first seventeen buildings having been sold. Three new buildings with more than a hundred offices and exhibition spaces are currently under construction.

For the district of Birkenfeld, the project has resulted in direct investments of millions of euros for local contractors. It has provided an important trading center not only for Chinese who wanted to enter the local market, but also for German companies that were looking for contacts in China. And, even though the Birkenfeld district is a rural location, it has proven very advantageous for the Chinese. They can travel by train to Paris in only three hours and can also reach the Hunsrück-Hahn Airport (formerly the U.S. Air Force's Hahn Air Base) by car in forty-five minutes. The international airport at Frankfurt am Main is a one-and-a half-hour drive.

The Hunsrück Region

Then, in 2015, a new national park was established in the area. The Hunsrück-Hochwald (high forest) National Park now protects roughly twenty-five thousand acres of upland forests and fields with nature-based tourism activities that include hiking and guided tours along with various child- and family-friendly facilities, such as summer toboggan runs and many walking and cycling opportunities.

The Erbeskopf mountain, the location of the SOC III radar and microwave relay station at the highest point in the Hunsrück, now provides a ski resort that has three slopes of twenty-six hundred feet and fifteen hundred feet in length. In the cooler months, fully automatic snow machines generate enough snow on the slopes to offer an extended ski season. Ski and snowboard rentals, a ski and snowboarding school and catering facilities are available on site.

* * *

It is a credit to the people of the now united Germany, and particularly to the residents in the district of Birkenfeld and its surrounding villages, that the Hunsrück area has emerged from the Cold War as a thriving, productive center for education, tourism and international commerce.

After centuries of domination by military occupations before and during the wars of the twentieth century, the people of the Hunsrück are no longer so strongly influenced by the presence and demands of military forces in Europe. They now have more freedom to pursue the real challenges of life and are able to enjoy the rewards of their efforts to achieve a higher purpose than provide a military fortification zone.

The United States has certainly played an important part in the restoration of Germany through its economic support and the military defense of its sovereignty after World War II.

Nuclear Weapons Reduction

In 1986, NATO decided that ninety-six cruise missiles, fitted with nuclear warheads, would be stored at Pydna, an American missile base in Kastellaun, Germany, about forty-four miles from Neubrücke. A lesser amount of nuclear-equipped Nike Hercules missiles had been stationed there previously when under SOC III control.

Then, in October 1986, at the marketplace in the nearby village of Bell, the largest demonstration in the Hunsrück's history took place. Around two hundred thousand people peacefully protested against the deployment of the missiles. At the end of the day's protest, the Hunsrück Declaration was read out to the crowd, calling for a reversal of NATO security policy. Fortunately, the deployment of the missiles never transpired due to the Cold War ending two years later, and the missile base was closed in August 1993.

The Pydna facility now hosts Nature One, considered one of the largest European open-air electronic music festivals. Facilities for the popular event use the same bunkers and infrastructure that once provided support to sixty-four ground-launch missiles and tactical nuclear missiles under the operational control of the U.S. Air Force.

In the 1980s, nuclear-capable Nike Hercules missiles began to be replaced by the higher-performance and more mobile Patriot missile. The Patriot's accuracy allowed it to be more effective without a nuclear warhead. As a result, the last Nike Hercules missiles were deactivated in Europe in 1988, without ever having been fired in anger – or in error! Changes in the U.S. defense posture in Europe followed the easing of Cold War tensions and had resulted in the reduction of the U.S. forward-deployed missile presence.

In September 1991, following the break-up of the Soviet Union, U.S. President George H. W. Bush (Bush Sr., 1989-1993) announced that the U.S. would, "eliminate all of its ground-launched short-range theater nuclear weapons; bring home and destroy all U.S. nuclear artillery shells and short-range ballistic missile warheads; and withdraw all tactical nuclear weapons from its ships and submarines, as well as all tactical nuclear weapons associated with U.S. land-based naval aircraft." While this constituted a remarkably positive move toward the defusing of nuclear tensions in Central Europe, it should be noted that this announcement did not call for the removal of the tactical nuclear weapons assigned to U.S. Air Force aircraft.

President Bush also announced that, "Many of these land- and sea-based warheads will be dismantled and destroyed. Those remaining will be secured in central areas where they would be available if necessary in a future crisis." He then called upon the Soviet leadership to reciprocate his unilateral efforts.

As a result, these initiatives led to a greater than eighty-five percent reduction in U.S. forward-deployed tactical nuclear weapons in Europe between 1991 and 1993. Perhaps no one noticed, but this may have been the best news to come out of Washington since the lunar touchdown of the American astronauts in 1969.

SECOND THOUGHTS

SINCE COMPLETING MY YEARS ON the Watch nearly fifty years ago, I have wanted to tell the story of what I had learned and experienced but had considered this data to be restricted from publication and perhaps just not that interesting to most people.

Then, in early 2016, a personal health emergency prompted an incident that brought me to the verge of departure from my body. As I lay in a medically induced coma for three days, I still sensed that there were many responsibilities for me to fulfill in this life. I was taken out of the coma as my body started to improve, and during my slow recovery I realized that I would have been remiss to pass away without relating this story to my family, my many friends and to all those who share a concern for the survival of mankind.

* * *

Unfortunately, the story of the military occupation in western Germany is not over. Though diminished, the NATO military presence is still part of the opposing forces in the world that face off at fortified outposts in Asia, Europe, in the air and both on and under the oceans. Most importantly, this military presence consists of the worldwide deployment of nuclear weapons.

In 2012, the Obama Administration initiated the Life Extension Program for the B61 tactical nuclear weapon in Europe. Without close inspection, one might initially consider that the title of this program refers to the preservation of human life. But, of course, in the context of nuclear weapons, it actually refers to extending the life of the last tactical nuclear weapons for U.S. aircraft maintained in the European arsenal, hardly what I would call a positive step forward in human survival.

As of late 2013, there were only two hundred B61 nuclear weapons actively in use by the United States. Of these, one hundred and eighty have been deployed within Europe. This bomb has a one-third kiloton to three-hundred-and-forty-kiloton yield, depending on versions and settings. A three-hundred-and forty-kiloton bomb is capable of more than twenty-two times the force of the bomb dropped on Hiroshima.

So, with a potential of one hundred and eighty B61 bombs poised to be launched in Europe, the Life Extension Program provides a total destructive force that is nearly four thousand times greater than the Hiroshima blast of 1945.

The explanation for continuing to maintain the U.S. nuclear presence in Europe has been stated as a need for these weapons to "contribute to the cohesion of the alliance," and that it is "critical for transatlantic security." This is certainly a creative construction of positive concepts to gain support for a particularly dangerous political and military stance that could result in an escalation of nuclear warfare: a level of force that could lead to the devastation of Europe and the spread of illness and destruction to the populations and ecosystems of Earth. A peculiar understanding of Life Extension.

Further investigation into the current status of nuclear weapons on Earth reveals that nine countries together possess around fifteen thousand nuclear weapons. This is according to a study published in 2017 by the Federation of American Scientists, a non-profit organization with the stated purpose of using science and scientific analysis to attempt to make the world more secure.

The U.S. and Russia, while each having proclaimed that they are no longer engaged in a Cold War, maintain a combined total of about eighteen hundred nuclear weapons on high-alert status, ready to be launched within minutes of warning. Their combined stockpiles of nuclear weapons comprise more than ninety percent of the total of such weapons on Earth.

Eighteen hundred nuclear weapons strategically deployed on high-alert status. No Cold War here!

The United States (6,800 warheads) spends more on its nuclear arsenal than all other countries combined.

The scope of the problem becomes more complex in view of the fact that five European nations host U.S. nuclear weapons as part of the NATO nuclear-sharing arrangement, and roughly two dozen other nations rely on U.S. nuclear weapons for their security.

Not to be outdone in the contest of East versus West, Russia (7,000 warheads) has the largest arsenal and is presently investing heavily in modernizing its warheads and delivery systems.

And, of course, along with the U.S., the powerful Western alliance still standing in opposition to Russia consists of The United Kingdom (215 warheads) maintaining a fleet of four nuclear-armed submarines in

Scotland, each carrying sixteen missiles and France (300 warheads) having most of its nuclear warheads deployed on submarines, with one boat on continuous patrol and some warheads deliverable by aircraft.

This gives a grand total of more than seven thousand and three hundred nuclear weapons in the hands of the NATO countries standing in readiness to oppose the primary military forces of the former Soviet Union, with Russia maintaining its seven thousand nuclear weapons. Perhaps not a Cold War, but distinctly on the chilly side!

In the early 1960s, the concept of Mutually Assured Destruction (appropriately labeled MAD by its proponents, oddly enough, and its detractors) gained acceptance as the primary U.S. military strategy and national security policy regarding nuclear weapons.

During the Kennedy administration of the early 1960s, Secretary of Defense Robert McNamara (yes, that same instigator of the Vietnam War) first outlined the theory of a flexible nuclear response that called for the stockpiling of a huge nuclear arsenal. The strategy was intended to provide a tense but stable global peace.

He theorized that in the event of a Soviet attack, the U.S. should have sufficient nuclear firepower to survive the first wave of nuclear strikes from the Soviets and be able to strike back immediately. The U.S. response would be so massive that the enemy would suffer "assured destruction."

This doctrine was bought into and promoted by U.S. politicians and military leaders, and the American public accepted the practical "wisdom" of this strategy. The resultant "arms race" had satisfied military and industrial demands for expansion and stimulated economic growth through enormous expenditures on its nuclear weapons program. During the years from 1940 through 1996, the

U.S. had spent an estimated minimum of *five and a half trillion dollars* on these weapons.

The philosophy of nuclear deterrence had been established and is still in play. The MAD doctrine assumed that each side had enough nuclear weapons to destroy the other side and that either side, if attacked for any reason by the other, would retaliate without fail with equal or greater force. The expected result would be an immediate, irreversible escalation of hostilities resulting in both combatants' mutual, total and assured destruction. Apparently, the rules of the game had now been written and would be carried out by the inmates in the asylum.

As McNamara pointed out, "The conclusion, then, is clear: if the United States is to deter a nuclear attack on itself or its allies, it must possess an actual and a credible assured-destruction capability." If the other side knew that initiating a nuclear strike would inevitably lead to its own destruction, it would be irrational to press the button. And most of us who have cared to look are all well aware of the high level of rationality that our world leaders have demonstrated throughout history.

The MAD principle does not take into account such suicidal national tendencies as those shown by Japan in World War II clearly displayed when it simultaneously initiated military aggression against the U.S. and England.

MAD has been seen as a means to prevent any direct full-scale conflicts between the U.S. and the Soviet Union while they engaged in smaller proxy wars around the world, such as the fabricated war in Vietnam. It was also responsible for the arms race, as both nations struggled to keep nuclear parity, or at least retain second-strike capability.

In November of 1967, privately concluding that the Vietnam War was futile, Robert Strange McNamara (that's his full name; I couldn't make that up) announced his resignation from the Secretary of Defense post. He then became President of the World Bank, an international financial institution that provides loans to promote economic and social programs in developing countries. McNamara presided over the World Bank for thirteen years. One can only wonder what mischief the creator of the MAD doctrine and architect of the Vietnam War accomplished in the sphere of international economics during his lengthy tenure.

Although the Cold War was announced to be ended in the early 1990s, the MAD doctrine continues to be applied and seems to have lulled all sides into a stable global peace, oblivious to the consequences of a nuclear conflict. Today, the notion of all-out nuclear war is considered a threat from another age; that it could never happen in today's more enlightened international diplomatic scene.

Of course, the MAD doctrine is essentially flawed in that it does not take into account imperfect policies and procedures, human error, system malfunctions, irrational behavior of military personnel and delusional or psychopathic national leaderships, and a host of other variables that might result in unintended weapon launches.

Malfunctions in equipment or procedures might erroneously detect a launch by the other side. In the modern world of reliance on computers, we are all well aware of computer glitches, system failures and malicious hacker intrusions. Faulty equipment or accidental battle station orders could lead to a full nuclear exchange. As an example, the 1983 case of the Soviet defense system malfunction that displayed an incoming U.S. nuclear missile attack would have resulted in Soviet retaliation if not correctly evaluated and reported by Soviet officer Stanislav Petrov.

Rogue or misinformed military commanders might have the ability to corrupt the launch decision process. As mentioned earlier in this book, this almost occurred during the Cuban Missile Crisis when a Soviet nuclear-armed submarine that had been cut off from radio communication commenced to deploy nuclear weapons. Fortunately, the second-in-command, Vasili Arkhipov, refused to launch the nuclear weapons despite the order from his senior officer to do so.

Nuclear delivery systems that rely on the superior analytical judgments and good intentions of military personnel responsible for their deployment and release should not be considered to be systems that are under control. I have wondered over the years how many other nuclear "close calls" have been avoided, how many other heroes we should thank for their acts of salvation from the consequences of a mishap or misunderstanding.

To protect us from immediate harm, all leaders with nuclear launch capability would first need to ensure that they hold the survival of their subjects as their primary role even when misled or deluded into response to a real or imaginary threat. As Winston Churchill warned, there is no strategy that will "cover the case of lunatics or dictators in the mood of Hitler when he found himself in his final dugout."

Which brings us to the smaller participants in the Nuclear Club, the presumably unallied individual nations rattling their nuclear sabers for whatever value they hope to gain from threats and intimidation of their neighbors.

Greatest in quantity among those is China (270 warheads) able to deliver by air, land and sea. India (110–120 warheads) has developed nuclear weapons in breach of its non-proliferation agreements, as they stand ready to oppose Pakistan (120–130 warheads) that is making regular improvements to and increasing the size of its nuclear arsenal and infrastructure.

Israel (80 warheads) has neither confirmed nor denied the existence of its nuclear arsenal, while North Korea (10 warheads) has shouted out to the world that it is prepared to defend itself through a preemptive launch against the U.S. with an arsenal of probably ten warheads and an expanding delivery capability that is being pursued very actively.

The failure of the major nuclear powers to actually disarm after declaring an end to the Cold War has heightened the risk that other countries will attempt to emulate the superpowers through the development and acquisition of nuclear weapons. This has been demonstrated in the number of nations that have become members of the Nuclear Club since the end of the Cold War.

Who will be next to join the "mighty" nations that wield these horrific weapons? The only guarantee against the further spread and ultimate use of nuclear weapons is for the major players to begin eliminating these weapons without delay.

Although many leaders of some nuclear-armed nations have expressed their vision of a nuclear-weapon-free world, they have failed to develop any detailed and workable plans to eliminate their arsenals and are actually modernizing them to make their war machines more efficient.

But this has not escaped notice from those who have committed themselves to heading off a future nuclear disaster with their concerted efforts for the negotiation of a nuclear weapon ban treaty by all the countries of Earth.

The International Campaign to Abolish Nuclear Weapons (ICAN) is a coalition of non-governmental organizations in one hundred countries promoting adherence to and implementation of the United Nations nuclear weapon ban treaty adopted in New York City in July 2017.

In recognition of these efforts, in October 2017 ICAN was awarded the Nobel Peace Prize. A spokesperson of the UN Secretary-General stated, "This Prize recognizes the determined efforts of civil society to highlight the unconscionable humanitarian and environmental consequences that would result if [nuclear weapons] were ever used again."

ICAN had successfully lobbied for the UN General Assembly to adopt a resolution in December 2016 to commence negotiations on a legally binding agreement to prohibit nuclear weapons – heralding an end to two decades of stalled progress in nuclear disarmament efforts. ICAN has worked with governments to achieve a strong and effective treaty. To date, around two-thirds of the world's nations have voted in favor of adopting the resolution.

As a result of the earlier Comprehensive Nuclear-Test-Ban Treaty (CTBT) that prohibits all nuclear explosions, the United States conducted its last nuclear test in 1992. Both Russia and China halted nuclear testing as a result of the CTBT, and only North Korea has conducted nuclear tests since 1998. The Test-Ban Treaty was an important and necessary first step toward the elimination of all nuclear arsenals. So, we have been heading in the right direction.

In the meantime, let us hope that those who have been entrusted with the control of these weapons will consider the consequences of unleashing such forces, and that they will hesitate to destroy themselves and their fellow humans in their desperate need for any real or imagined security. And that those who will lead us into the future will show the wisdom to forbid the possession of such weapons by all governments of Earth.

The very existence of nuclear weapons invites disaster and destruction on the people of Earth. With even a small number of these weapons being dropped mistakenly or intentionally, human life on Earth could expire through the pollution effects of radiation with populations succumbing to widespread illnesses, without sufficient healing resources resulting in the end of human civilization, starting with a bang but ending in a drawn-out and painful whimper for most life forms.

The mere knowledge of the existence of nuclear weapons has long sent a continuous message to the populations of Earth that we are all susceptible to a discontinuation of our lives. Along with unexplained tiredness and physical exhaustion, a kind of hysteria sets in with the loss of hope for the future. One's body, family, home and worldly possessions might now be placed in jeopardy. In an actual nuclear conflict, there will be no "duck and cover" under the classroom desk with a return to school the next morning.

With the knowledge of an impending dangerous situation, particularly when it poses a threat to mankind, it is incumbent upon us all to encourage others to do something about it in a positive and practical way.

Support to ICAN or to any of the other hundred and thirty disarmament groups across the planet would enable them to increase awareness and education about the effects of nuclear weapons which just might result in a demand from the peoples of Earth to eliminate the threat of annihilation. ICAN can be supported through its website at http://nuclearban.org/the-campaign/

Sane and rational contemplation of the problem and resulting effective solutions in the matter of nuclear weapons are possible among world leaders. They should be appealed to and encouraged to act in favor of a planetary ban. They can be encouraged to support and implement real solutions that remove the threat of nuclear war and the hidden influences of threats that have hung over us for many decades.

Despite occasional deviations from its leadership role in the world, such as the actions taken in its catastrophic involvement in Vietnam, the U.S. has long provided a strong message to the world that all people are created equal and that they are entitled to the inalienable rights of life, liberty and the pursuit of happiness. The U.S. now needs to step forward and take full responsibility for having developed nuclear weapons and assume a leadership position in the removal and elimination of the most powerful weapons ever developed and unleashed on planet Earth.

That will require a strong and compassionate leadership that embraces an unflinching dedication to the concept of safeguarding life on Earth and the pursuit of happiness for all mankind. Such a leadership will certainly be worthy of the greatest admiration and respect ever bestowed on a member of human society.

Meanwhile, we all need to remain on the Watch to ensure the survival of mankind. Let's start by finding and supporting those with the courage to accomplish the task of prohibiting nuclear weapons on our planet!

ACKNOWLEDGMENTS

I WOULD LIKE TO EXPRESS appreciation to my son Jed Rigney and my daughter Evie Rigney Blazek who have managed my graphic design business during the time of my convalescence, enabling me to research and write this book with minimum distraction.

I would like to offer special thanks to my son Bret Rigney who provided the explanatory illustrations and the artwork for both covers of this book. I am also grateful for the assistance given by Alex Irving, John and Diane Lichtensteiger, my wife Chris Rigney and my son Jed for their review and suggested amendments to the final manuscript. And thanks to James Callaghan for his assistance in the typesetting and final layout of the publishing files. Despite the assistance of the above, all errors, oversights or inaccuracies are, of course, solely my responsibility.

I am especially grateful for the support and encouragement given by my wife Chris who has shared her life with me for the past fifty years, from the moment when I first met her as the attractive and optimistic Army nurse who had taken on the improbable task of cultivating a tropical plant on a mountain range in Germany and who still tolerates and occasionally expresses much-appreciated amusement at my sometimes lame attempts at humor.

Lightning Source UK Ltd.
Milton Keynes UK
UKHW021849260420
362350UK00015B/137